Praise for Threadbare

"*Threadbare* takes us down the rabbit hole of the global fashion and textile industries, connecting the dots between the lives of the women who work at Forever 21 and the women who sew the clothes that hang on the racks there. With vivid storytelling and deep investigation. Anne Elizabeth Moore and her team of talented cartoonists prove the strength of comics as a tool for translating impossible complexity to our everyday experience." —Jessica Abel, author of *Out on the Wire, La Perdida,* and *Drawing Words & Writing Pictures*

"A fascinating look into the lives behind our clothes. From the people who make them, to the people who model them, to the people who sell them, our clothes are part of an intricate network which spans the globe. The art in *Threadbare* helps draw a personal connection to what might otherwise be overwhelming statistics, and gives an intimate look into the way the world is affected by what we buy." —Sarah Glidden, author of *Rolling Blackouts* and *How to Understand Israel in 60 Days or Less*

"*Threadbare* is a brilliant amalgam of art, storytelling, consciousness-building, and old-fashioned muckraking. It takes on the enormous project of confronting the international apparel trade, through delving into individual stories and lifting up voices that are usually suppressed or ignored in mass media. The Ladydrawers collective and Anne Elizabeth Moore bring us face to face, literally, with the people most affected by labor exploitation and abuse—and in seeing their faces, we understand the realities beyond the facts. An intrepid journey!" —Maya Schenwar, editor-in-chief of *Truthout* and author of *Locked Down, Locked Out: Why Prison Doesn't Work and How We Can Do Better*

"Describing the environmental, social, economic and personal costs of fast fashion in a style cool as gin, *Threadbare* is both a damning indictment and a stellar example of comics journalism." —Molly Crabapple, author of *Drawing Blood*

"A compelling and comprehensive portrai͏͏   ͏͏ͪuman cost behind what we wear. The sharp, gorgeous, and distressing *Thr͏͏*   ͏͏questioning both your wardrobe and the state of the worl͏͏   ͏͏ͭhor of *Investigating Lois Lane* and *Wonder Wo͏͏*

"Well-researched, engaging, and full of ͏͏.   ͏͏) statistics, you may finish reading this book and decide to be͏͏͏͏   ͏͏ger shop-ping for clothes at your local mall and pressuring your electe͏͏   ͏͏legislation that holds clothing manufacturers and retailers responsible." —Lisa Wilde, author of *Yo, Miss: A Graphic Look at High School*

"Colleges offering degree programs in fashion need to add this book to the curriculum. A must read!!!!" —Carol Tyler, author of *Late Bloomer* and *You'll Never Know*

Praise for the Ladydrawers Comics Collective

"Wry."—*New York Times Magazine*

"Beautifully illustrated intellectual ammunition." —*ThinkProgress*

"Depressing news, but the comic makes it a little easier to swallow." —*Bitch*

"Making an art form out of researching and publishing findings that others might write or talk about." —*Forbes*

Praise for Anne Elizabeth Moore

"One of the sharpest thinkers and cultural critics bouncing around the globe today." —*Razorcake*

"Notable underground author." —*The Onion*

"Anne Elizabeth Moore lets readers peer over her shoulder as she attempts the implausible. It turns out, the implausible is hard, and funny, and tragic, and illuminating, but once you sign up for the journey she never lets you look away." —Glynn Washington, NPR's *Snap Judgment*

"A post-Empirical, proto-fourth-wave-feminist memoir-cum-academic abstract that makes our country's Mommy Wars look like child's play and proves why we should be paying attention to Cambodia's record of human rights and gender equity." —*Bust Magazine* (reviewing *New Girl Law*)

"Attains the modest yet important success of making personal narratives and experience matter to critiques of history and globalization." —*Hyphen Magazine* (reviewing *Cambodian Grrrl*)

Threadbare

Clothes, Sex & Trafficking

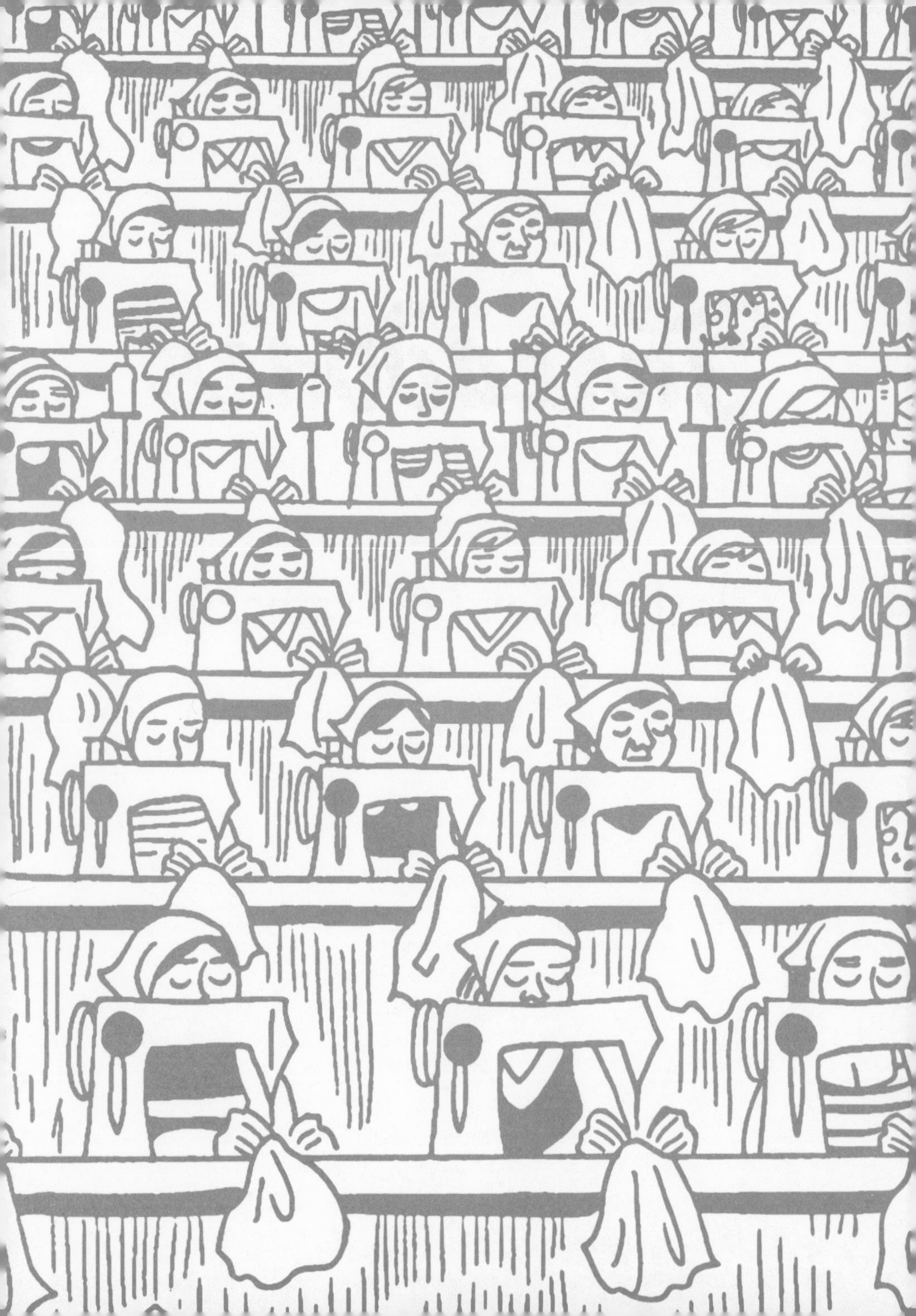

Threadbare

Clothes, Sex & Trafficking

Anne Elizabeth Moore
& the Ladydrawers

Microcosm Publishing
Portland, Oregon

THREADBARE
Clothes, Sex, and Trafficking

All text and artwork © Anne Elizabeth Moore and individual creators, 2016
This edition © Microcosm Publishing, 2016

Cover illustration by Meggyn Pomerleau
Cover design by Joe Biel
Book design by Joe Biel and Elly Blue

Art on inside covers and pages 4, 5, 93, and 101 by Ellen Lindner
Art on page 28 by Julia Gfrörer
Art on page 48 by Delia Jean
Art on pages 47 and 67 by Simon Häussle
Art on pages 81, 82, and 109 by Melissa Mendes
Art on page 110 by Leela Corman

ISBN 978-1-62106-739-9

First printing, May 10, 2016

This is Microcosm #254

Distributed worldwide by Legato / Perseus and in the UK by Turnaround
This book was printed on post-consumer paper in the United States.

Library of Congress Cataloging-in-Publication Data:

Moore, Anne Elizabeth, author.
Threadbare : clothes, sex, and trafficking / by Anne Elizabeth Moore ;
    illustrated by the Ladydrawers.
First edition. | Portland, Oregon : Microcosm Publishing, 2016.
    | Includes bibliographical references.
LCCN 2015038891 | ISBN 9781621067399 (pbk.)
LCSH: Clothing trade--Moral and ethical aspects--Comic books,
    strips, etc. | Women clothing workers--Comic books, strips, etc. | Unfair
    labor practices--Comic books, strips, etc. | Human trafficking--Comic
    books, strips, etc. | Graphic novels.
LCC HD9940.A2 M656 2016 | DDC 364.15/51--dc23
LC record available at http://lccn.loc.gov/2015038891

For a catalog, write:

Microcosm Publishing
2752 N. Williams Ave
Portland, OR 97227

or visit MicrocosmPublishing.com

Table of Contents

Chapter Three: Cambodia

Chapter Four: The World

Acknowledgements

The list of various collaborators involved in the creation of this book barely hints at the full roster of folks whose talents, thoughtfulness, humor, and intelligence was put to use (and, at times, misuse) in the course of creating it. Indeed, Leela Corman, Julia Gfrörer, Simon Häussle, Delia Jean, Ellen Lindner, and Melissa Mendes were a joy to work with as contributors; Delia Jean and Melissa Mendes are also regular participants in many Ladydrawers projects and working with them is often what makes difficult subjects palatable (or even fun). R. Swanson, Morgan Claire Siréne, Sheika Lugtu, Fran Kang, Laura Ķeniņš, and Lindsey Smith also perform the daily grind of comicking, cat-petting, and general superheroics that all go into a typical Ladydrawers day. Although they are often more fully engaged in other projects, they must be considered among contributors to this volume. Then there is the *Truthout* crew: Joe Macaré, Maya Schenwar, and Leslie Thatcher, in particular, who supported this inquiry from day one with enthusiasm and the appropriate amount of guidance. Not to mention the many subjects who allowed me to query them at length, who are depicted herein for your viewing pleasure.

In Cambodia, I am lucky to have friends at the *Cambodia Daily*, Paññāsāstra University of Cambodia, the Harpswell Foundation, and spread throughout the country, who have offered invaluable assistance in support of my continued work there. Simon Marks, the reporter behind the *Newsweek* story on Somaly Mam and many of the earlier reports of fraud in her organizations, deserves an intellectual hat-tip. A theorist-in-residence program at das weisse haus in Vienna supported my research throughout Austria; Wiebke Miljes was particularly assistive in all matters. Additionally, the Puntigam clan, based in Vienna, as well as their friends, families, and future generations, offered overwhelming support for this project, from the suggestion that I look into Marienthal to the frequent dinner experiments I forced them to endure—and invent!—as my diet shifted. Back in Chicago, Nick and Nadine deserve a similar nod: thank you sincerely for putting up with my insane diet with aplomb.

Finally, a special nod to the Propeller Fund, an innovative, collaborative arts regranting program supported by the Andy Warhol Foundation and threewalls, who generously offered the funds that allowed us to put out this book with the delightful but underfunded Microcosm Publishing.

—Anne Elizabeth Moore
Chicago, 2016

Foreword

The book that eventually became *Threadbare: Clothes, Sex, and Trafficking* was originally a monthly comics journalism series, planned as a way to paint a clear image of the otherwise impossible-to-picture international apparel trade. The garment industry employs between one sixth and one seventh of all women on earth, and therefore is probably the single-most responsible entity for the global gender wage gap. Over the two years that the strips took, start to finish, to investigate, research, write, draw, edit, and have published on *Truthout* (not counting the extra year to polish the strips for print and put together the book itself) the project became much bigger than that. Sort of. Or the global garment trade did. What I discovered early on was that the apparel industry seeps uncomfortably quickly into larger issues of women's job options and poverty, and raises serious questions about how we talk about and respond to the issue we now call human trafficking. From there, the leakage oozes further: the garment industry plays a significant but complicated role in how we define and legislate sex work—around the world and here in the U.S. All told, the apparel industry has a much stronger hold over women's economic and migratory freedoms worldwide than we have so far been able to comprehend. This book, however, will draw you a clear picture.

When I first proposed it as a series, I had no idea the story was so massive. Even on a smaller scale, I wasn't sure it would be possible to access and depict the entirety of the garment trade in monthly installments, although I had been reporting on the garment industry in Cambodia for several years by then. Depicting a global industry in comics form would take a lot of travel, to name just one hurdle to completing the strips, and most of the truly great comics artists I know prefer to work on fiction. It's also rare for a news site to agree to such a project: an investigative comics journalism series is, ah, unconventional on the best of days. Not to mention that an open-ended investigative series that seeks to explore and portray the unimaginable mess that the garment industry has become in recent decades is basically impossible, and my desire to cast in clean line and sparse prose the havoc that the clothes we wear wreak on everyone who works the supply chain—from models to warehousers, from retail employees to sewers—was equally Sisyphean. In creation, display, distribution, sales, and consumption, our clothes are keeping women in poverty around the world. We may sense it instinctually, but I wanted to show it. The task I set out for this project was to draw a concise image of something we cannot see, articulate systems we cannot envision, and share information to which we often simply do not have access.

Compared to the ridiculousness of the task, however, working with editor Leslie Thatcher was a dream. Each strip elicited praise, thoughtful grammatical suggestions, and a handful of enthusiastic emoticons. More than that, even, the opportunity to offer a modest amount of pay to comics creators on a monthly basis for investigative non-fiction remains to this day nearly unheard of in U.S. media. Without it, this book would not have been possible; neither would it have emerged without the incredible talents of all the artists involved, whose profoundly diverse approaches to image-making and fact-configuring lend this narrative the range of styles that a truly global tale requires.

We've divided our story into four chapters, each named for the primary region where particular aspects of our tale can be located. The United States is home, of course, to the display, retail, distribution, and importing machinations of apparel, and Delia Jean, Julia Gfrörer, Melissa Mendes, and I show you in the first chapter how U.S. workers are affected by the global apparel industry.

Europe's role in the garment trade is similar to that of the U.S., so instead of focusing on production, we thought we'd talk a bit about how men—consumers, primarily—fit into the apparel industry. For this task, we went to Austria, a place with a formerly thriving garment industry now chock full of fast-fashion outlets. (The nation has the same population as the city of Chicago but nearly 21 times as many H&M retail stores.)

Many of the clothes Austrian men purchase today, therefore, are produced in Asia—often South or Southeast Asia—and the largely female workforce is drastically underpaid, at an often paltry percentage of a living wage. Women workers cannot always make ends meet, although few other employment options exist. To feed babies, make rent, or survive, many women enter the sex trade—a good number, it turns out, do so at will. Anti-sex-trafficking NGOs often fail to acknowledge this truth, however. They also overlook that workers are being forced into so-called rehabilitation programs they may not want (which occasionally includes religious conversion that is not always at-will). Indeed, the "rehabilitation" program many NGOs offer amounts to training for the exact same garment industry positions many had left in the first place, although at a slim fraction of the pay they'd get in the factories (which is already, of course, a narrow portion of what is required to live on). That the garment industry funds many of these NGOs may strike readers as responsible. However the end result is a large-scale system of international policies that, on the ground, restrict women's employment options around the world. Seeing the ways that similar policies with the same intentions are being implemented here in the U.S, even though they stand in violation of the human rights of women workers, may allow you to comprehend the role clothing plays in our daily lives in a whole new way.

It's an expansive story. To help ground it, I'll share a brief introduction at the top of each chapter with some background information; the endnotes have all been collected following the strips in each section.

However big this tale gets, it's still growing. The global garment trade is overproducing at such an alarming rate that it's no longer just the workers who can't keep up (see Chapter Three): consumers can no longer keep pace either, and I'll share an anecdote to prove my point.

It begins with the precarious stack of clothes I'd purchased over the first year of research, primarily to get questions answered by store workers during checkout. A year to the day after the first strip appeared, I decided to return them, and hauled a staggering pile of clothes to the Forever 21 on State Street in Chicago. There I was quickly informed of a new policy regarding returns: they must go through the multi-floor retail outlet next door to the one I was currently standing in, named XXI Forever. I would describe XXI Forever as a down-market version of Forever 21 if the upscale version weren't equally jam-packed with the garishly colored, tight-fitting clothes favored by teenagers (and, OK, me) but XXI Forever had even more clothes, in more colors, and I quickly felt overwhelmed.

(As an aside to the anecdote, I was a bit south of the H&M where, in 2010, the truly global effects of the garment trade had first dawned on me— when, in fact, I first started thinking about the project that would eventually become this book. I had been writing at the time on a series of bizarre mass faintings in Cambodia that were blamed variously on chemical leaks, mass hysteria, and ghosts; in fact, as I wrote for *Truthout*, women were fainting because they were doing more work than the industry had ever before required. I was at that H&M in 2010 when I met a group of retail workers who had just left their jobs en masse, they told me, because keeping up with the ever-quickening pace of retail—getting new lines out on the floor every day, removing the old ones, sending them who-knows-where—and a faulty air-conditioning unit had caused them all to faint on the job during the summer heat wave. Obviously, laborers at no point along the production, distribution, or sales line could reliably keep up with the demands of manufacturing any longer. This was as clear to me in downtown Chicago as it had been in Phnom Penh.)

Representatives of the garment industry explain that consumers are behind the ever-quickening pace of fast fashion. But as I stood inside XXI Forever, a four-story, deep-discount sibling retail outlet of an already discounted four-floor store a door south, it became clear that this wasn't true either. For the dozen or so items I wished to return to XXI Forever could only be traded in, and the store had a strict BOGO policy: Buy One, Get One Free. This means that the 12 items I had but did not need could only be returned by trading them in for 24 different, new items; I tried, of course, to eschew the "One Free" I didn't need. Not allowed. (Everyone I knew got glittery spangles as holiday gifts that year.)

The garment industry, it seems, is now inventing ways to give this stuff away. Meanwhile, women around the world are being arrested, imprisoned, and coerced into entering the industry, no matter how little it pays. It's a system that's wearing thin. Shouldn't we get rid of it?

—Anne Elizabeth Moore, Chicago

Chapter 1:
The United States

If the United States isn't the birthplace of fast fashion, it is certainly its spiritual home and primary beneficiary. Named for and based on the concept of fast food (in which cheap and easy hot meals are always available to the consumer, with a limited array of modifications), fast fashion has sought to make stylish but affordable clothing available to the consumer, created in a set palette of styles, patterns, and designs. A major difference between fast food and fast fashion, however, is that when the former is consumed, it's actually gone. Fast fashion would never have taken off if the clothing it produced could only be worn once; instead it was made "rare" (and nearly disposable). Designs and styles would be sold for only a limited time, and social pressure to stay on trend—plus quick construction and cheap materials—would do the rest, a solution that doubled as a revolutionary marketing strategy. This meant that the traditional four seasons of fashion quickly gave way to an ever-replenishing stock of affordable clothes. Inditex (Spanish owner of Zara stores and a few other outlets) paved the way for these industry-wide changes, although the Gap, Nike, Mango, Forever 21, H&M, and many others quickly followed suit, speeding up production lines, streamlining designs, and pushing new apparel items out the door in as few as six weeks.

That's where *Threadbare* begins. An introductory strip with Julia Gfrörer explains how the changes fast fashion set in motion at every stage of the apparel industry—from display to warehousing, from retail to policy—turned an in-home pursuit into an unfathomably vast industry in just about a hundred years. In that time, the garment industry has become the entity that most deserves to be taken to task for the global gender wage gap, although the poverty it inflicts isn't visible in the ads. Fashion advertising depicts women as carefree, thoughtless consumers. They may be independently wealthy; they may not be. They don't even care! The image projected by the fashion industry is that economics simply do not matter, but any fashion model—overworked, underpaid, and often as malnourished as a garment factory employee—will tell you otherwise. I lucked out by getting to spend a little time with Sarah Meier, an eloquent former supermodel, whose thoughtful takes on race, gender, sexuality, and economics in the modeling world set the tone for *Threadbare*. This is the debut of "Model Employee," drawn by Delia Jean, the first of the strips created exclusively for this book. (You'll want to note, for later, how seamlessly Meier addresses similarities between modeling and sex trafficking, nearly as an aside.)

Of course, the billboards, taxi signs, and print ads that are the output of models' underpaid labor offer most consumers their first awareness of fashion as an industry. To work, ads must convince you to visit a store, where you will be bombarded immediately with demands to shop now, and to return soon to shop again. Gfrörer's frenetic linework in "Let's Go Shopping" captures both the appeal of fast fashion and its crass, unseemly underbelly. She brings the same frantic pace to "The Business of Thrift," in which fast fashion's embrace of throwaway culture proves to be quite profitable for some.

Two strips drawn by Melissa Mendes finish out Chapter One, although they were originally slated to go to another artist. A scheduling conflict made for a last-minute substitution and my first collaboration with Mendes, who would go on to become my most frequent collaborator. The strip, too—"Zoned"— was enormously successful, as thousands upon thousands of readers shared our findings about shady Foreign Trade Zones, where so many of the products that enter the U.S. are housed for a short time. Of course, this is all laid out in a clear and above-board system of policy that Mendes and I explore in "Red Tape," which further looks at the bizarre connections our laws make between the apparel trade, terrorism, and intellectual property rights. Mendes's deeply silly underwire-inspecting officer with the Department of Homeland Security— covered in brassieres at the airport—belies the fundamentally troubling sense that the heavy regulations and surveillance aren't actually about terrorism at all.

FAST FASHION

WRITTEN BY ANNE ELIZABETH MOORE   DRAWN BY JULIA GFRÖRER

It started as a way to offer people fancy clothes for cheap...

...but fast fashion is also a way to get people to buy more of them

a LOT more.

A hundred years ago, the primary competition for mass-produced clothing was people's ability and inclination to sew it themselves.

$600 in today's dollars

Graceful Styles $20

Production was, at the time, largely domestic.

TRIANGLE SHIRTWAIST FACTORY FIRE, NEW YORK, USA. THE DEAD

...so when things went wrong at the factories...

...folks had recourse.

But as factory standard improved, the demand for mass-produced clothing grew.

$10

NEW LOOK

$175 in today's dollars

So, too, did the labor market.

The Multi-Fibre Agreement, introduced in 1974, offered developing nations order quotas from developed nations for entering the garment trade.

With smaller fingers and an interest in fashion...

...women were drawn to the emerging industry.

$19.99

$20 in today's dollars

In many developing nations, it gave women their first job opportunities

(It also made it easier to hide a factory's health and safety violations from consumers...

TAZREEN FASHION FACTORY FIRE, 2012 DHAKA, BANGLADESH 117 DEAD

...but we'll get back to that.)

The MFA ended in 2004 and industry analysts and fashion advocates world-wide thought it meant the end of the garment trade in developing nations.

The MFA had made garments cheaper to produce, for sure, and dropped prices.

Families were spending less on clothes, on average.

In 1901, a Massachusetts family earned $685 and spent $880 annually, 14% of which ($127) was spent on clothing.

A century later, earnings for a same-size family had grown to $57K, but only 4% ($1610) was spent on apparel every year. (1)

By 2004, the solution seemed to be...

abandon the tired old notion of seasonal clothing lines

① Quicken the turnaround between initial design and rack-ready wearables, and bring more product—and more consumers—in more often.

By 2005, Inditex had become one of the biggest fast fashion retailers—the second-largest worldwide—with $8 billion in sales. Now it's the largest, with $18.3 billion worth of sales last year. Worldwide, fast fashion is a $1.2 trillion industry, with $250 billion spent last year in the US alone. (2)

model employee

Sarah Meier——radio host, MTV VJ, model——was born in 1981 in Hong Kong and now lives in Manila.

I was expected to follow in her footsteps, but really chose to take [modeling] on, as an adult, at the age of 14, which is the prime age you're expected to start modeling. [That's when] I started getting agencies and a lot of castings.

Meier was based in New York, but moved back to the Philippines when she stopped modeling full-time. She was even announced to be the host of *Philippines Next Top Model* before the show was put on hiatus.

I did it for twelve years.

What did you enjoy about it?

[It's] one way of understanding who you are in the big picture ...

of understanding what role the model plays in the economy. I got to know a lot about business, and what businesses need and want.

I found myself in rooms with alot of really big decision-makers, and because I chose to network properly—not just get drunk, but really have decent conversations—I found that those relationships have proven fruitful. I've had business opportunities.

You have random places to stay when you're traveling around the world.

Then also, in a non-tangible way, I know what a really expensive car feels like to sit in. I know what it smells like. I know the feeling of being that beautifully dressed woman in high heels, and feeling really confident and being well made-up——I know what that feels like. Anywhere else along the journey in my life, I can still tap into that sometimes. I know what I want, I know what I like. I've tasted some really incredible food and seen some really beautiful places in the world, and I want to continue doing that.

Undereating is pervasive: Thirty-one percent of models who responded to a 2012 Model Alliance survey admitted to eating disorders. (3) Supermodel Amy Lemons was advised to eat only a rice cake a day. Others are offered more subtle hints, often backed up by contract stipulations, to lose inches from hips, thighs, or rear. (4)

First acknowledged in a 2008 *Vogue* article titled, "Is Fashion Racist?", the industry has struggled with accusations of racism since. The number of black models at New York's Spring Fashion Week hit a low in 2013, and the number of white models—83%—a high. By Fall Fashion Week 2014, the number of white models had dropped slightly to 79%, although this is still not technically "diverse." (5)

The Model Alliance report found that, of 85 surveys completed, over half the models surveyed had started between 13 and 16; another 1% had started earlier. (6)

The ones that have extremely strong ties to their childhood friends and family [come out of it OK]. They have a lot of guidance.

The ones that— sorry for my language—but the ones that really had their shit together were choosing bible study over clubs. It's hard to generalize, like, anybody that wasn't going to bible study was fucked, but it kind of seemed so.

Wherever your center was, if it wasn't stable or strong, the forces of the industry would suck girls up.

According to the Model Alliance, 68% of the workforce suffers from anxiety and/or depression. (7)

There was one girl I shared a model's apartment with. She was from somewhere down south and she had never seen the ocean before, so we brought her to Coney Island. She had tears streaming down her face. She wouldn't wear anything that exposed her belly.

I kept thinking, "How are you going to make it as a model in New York?" One part of me was like, "You've gotta conform a little bit," but another part of me wanted to protect her and be like, "Stay how you are. Go back to where you're from. The city's going to eat you alive."

You don't really get to talk about the girls that are coming out of this with eating disorders, or who feel like they need to use their sexuality to get anything in life. You see the chaos, the models scrambling to get dressed backstage at a fashion show...

... that's behind the scenes of the show, but behind the scenes of the life, that girl's going home and she's crying her eyes out because she's 16 and she misses her parents but she's too hell-bent on becoming popular to admit that to herself.

More than half of underage models, according to ModelAlliance, had never been or were only rarely accompanied by a legal guardian to castings or jobs. (8)

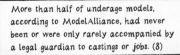

Or she's throwing up in the bathroom.

Or she's a country girl and she's getting her head shoved in some potful of cocaine and not knowing what the hell just happened.

A quarter of those surveyed by Model Alliance professed drug or alcohol dependency, and around a third lacked health insurance. (9)

Really really really nice girls turned into *horrible* creatures. When they moved in, everybody was a darling. Three months down the road, they're putting Nair in each other's shampoo bottles.

[Modeling] really draws out the core of whatever's ugly.

You could be looking at a blonde-haired, blue-eyed girl and you're not in competition at all, we're not going to be up for the same jobs ever. We're not even sent to the same castings. But the way in which we view each other is competition.

The animosity builds. It's not just animosity within the industry, for other models. It becomes animosity for anybody that's happy. Anybody that's living a normal life.

Not so many women come out of it feeling empowered, or confident, or having life skills to progress with anything other than their physical attributes.

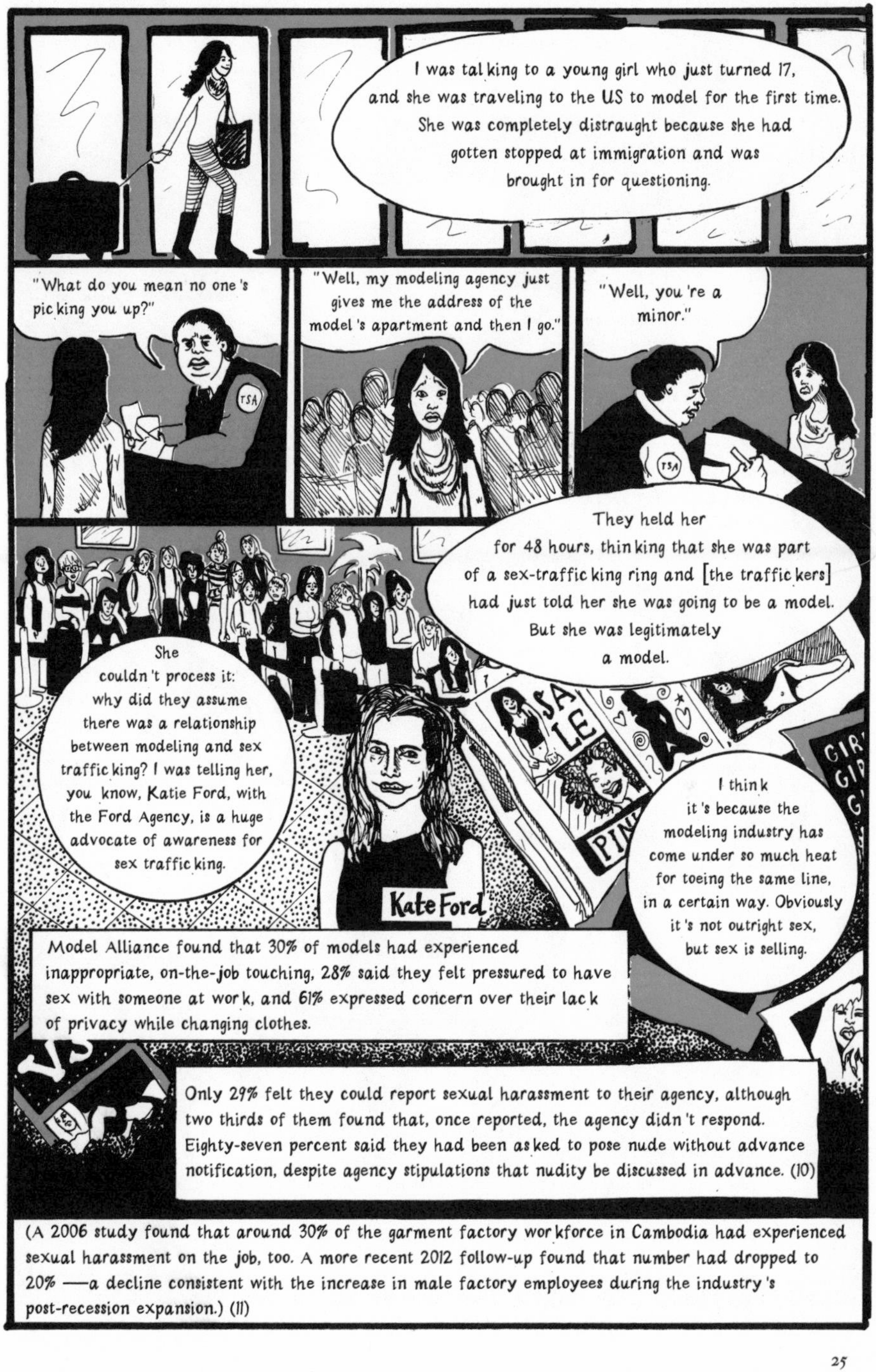
I was talking to a young girl who just turned 17, and she was traveling to the US to model for the first time. She was completely distraught because she had gotten stopped at immigration and was brought in for questioning.
"What do you mean no one's picking you up?"
TSA
"Well, my modeling agency just gives me the address of the model's apartment and then I go."
"Well, you're a minor."
TSA
They held her for 48 hours, thinking that she was part of a sex-trafficking ring and [the traffickers] had just told her she was going to be a model. But she was legitimately a model.
She couldn't process it: why did they assume there was a relationship between modeling and sex trafficking? I was telling her, you know, Katie Ford, with the Ford Agency, is a huge advocate of awareness for sex trafficking.
Kate Ford
SALE
I think it's because the modeling industry has come under so much heat for toeing the same line, in a certain way. Obviously it's not outright sex, but sex is selling.
Model Alliance found that 30% of models had experienced inappropriate, on-the-job touching, 28% said they felt pressured to have sex with someone at work, and 61% expressed concern over their lack of privacy while changing clothes.
Only 29% felt they could report sexual harassment to their agency, although two thirds of them found that, once reported, the agency didn't respond. Eighty-seven percent said they had been asked to pose nude without advance notification, despite agency stipulations that nudity be discussed in advance. (10)
(A 2006 study found that around 30% of the garment factory workforce in Cambodia had experienced sexual harassment on the job, too. A more recent 2012 follow-up found that number had dropped to 20% —a decline consistent with the increase in male factory employees during the industry's post-recession expansion.) (11)

Models are some of the most insecure people I know. Period. And that's not healed by becoming a more successful model. That's healed by *getting your ass out of it.* Completely.

How did you get out?

I got pregnant.

I thought it was the end of my life. I had six live endorsement contracts that had clauses stating that I was not to get pregnant—all the way down to that I was not to participate in premarital sex. If I were to be pregnant I was supposed to be married, but I wasn't even supposed to be married. I was supposed to stay single for the duration of this contract.

It's called a morality clause.

I was up to be sued for over a million dollars.

It turned out OK. I sat down with the clients one by one. I had been sitting in the boardroom crying my eyes out, but they brought me flowers and said, "Congratulations."

I gained 78 pounds while I was pregnant, and went back to New York to give birth.

When I came back here,

anybody that had known me as a model and saw me with all the weight gain ... the way they treated me was horrifying.

People walked straight past me—people I had gone on trips to Hong Kong with. They didn't even see me. Literally just walked right past. I'm smiling, about to say hi, and then the glance,

and then they pass.

It happened so frequently that I began to look for the polar opposite of whatever fulfillment modeling had given me. It was a lot of, like, I don't care how I look on the outside anymore, let me work on everything that was broken on the inside that was left malnourished, unattended.

It's easy to talk about now, but at the time it was my entire world. I felt like I had been raised by this industry, and then this was akin to your family shunning you because you gained some weight.

[My mom] is now a hermit. She is very reclusive. Anytime I tell her, "Oh momma I was at Fashion Week and so-and-so says hi," you can see her physically cringe. She'll make comments about how she looks old, she looks fat.

She's still skinnier than I am.

You can see the long-term effects. She's consumed by it ...

whatever "it" is.

Pay is also not what we'd expect. The US Bureau of Labor Statistics suggests models for clothing stores—in fast fashion—earned only around $19,300 in 2013, which breaks down to a mean hourly wage of $9.28 per hour. (12) That's just 83% of the current $11.50 per hour living wage in New York. (13) It's a higher percentage of the living wage than factory workers take home in most countries, but it's still a percentage of the living wage.

Some designers "pay" in "trade"—apparel that is often too small to sell to anyone else and not always hardy enough for everyday wear. Like factory workers, models regularly report wage theft (sometimes for reasons like weight gain) and delays of months, or years in receiving checks. Agencies also deduct fees for tests, visas, portfolios, delivery fees, and rent from earnings before payout, and not always tallied for workers' financial records.

WRITTEN BY:
Anne Elizabeth Moore
DRAWN BY:
DELIA JEAN

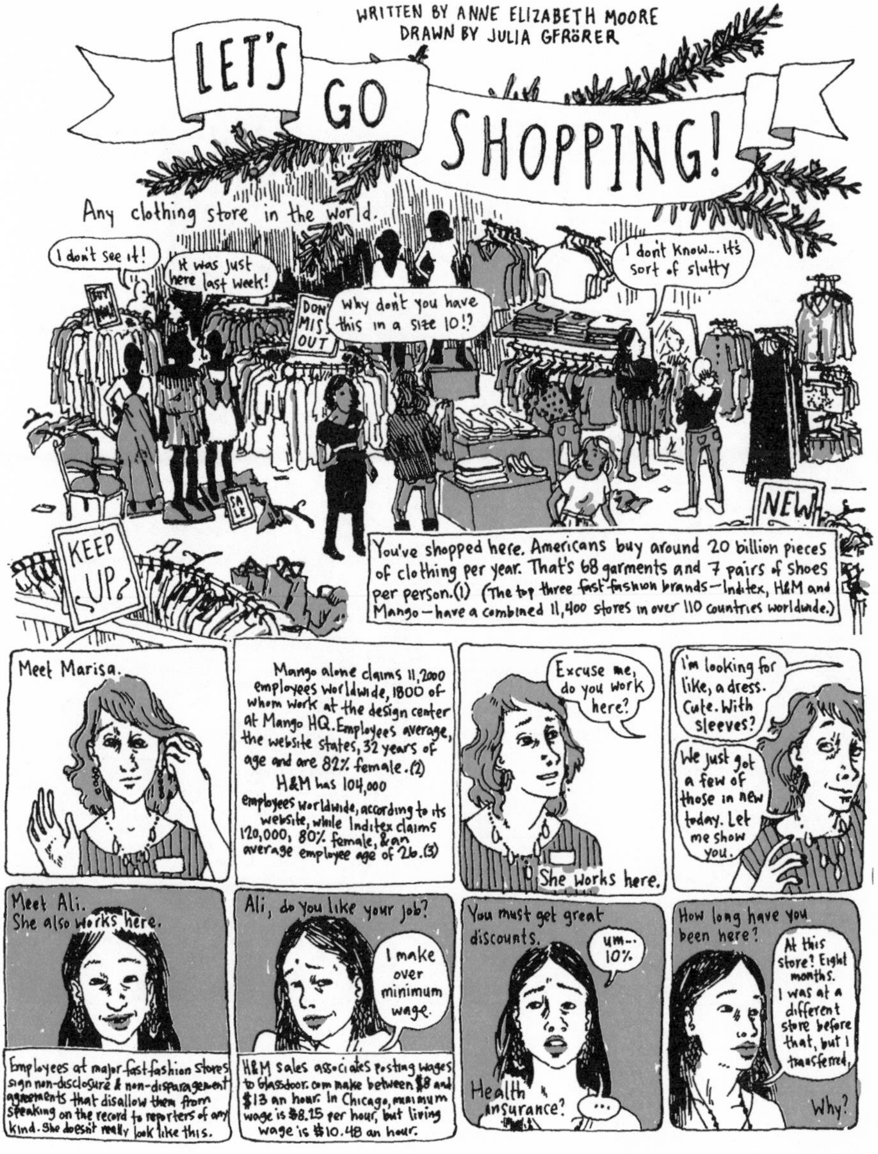
WRITTEN BY ANNE ELIZABETH MOORE
DRAWN BY JULIA GFRÖRER
LET'S GO SHOPPING!
Any clothing store in the world.
I don't see it!
It was just here last week!
DON'T MISS OUT
Why don't you have this in a size 10!?
I don't know... It's sort of slutty
SALE
NEW
KEEP UP
You've shopped here. Americans buy around 20 billion pieces of clothing per year. That's 68 garments and 7 pairs of shoes per person.(1) (The top three fast-fashion brands—Inditex, H&M and Mango—have a combined 11,400 stores in over 110 countries worldwide.)
Meet Marisa.
Mango alone claims 11,2000 employees worldwide, 1800 of whom work at the design center at Mango HQ. Employees average, the website states, 32 years of age and are 82% female.(2) H&M has 104,000 employees worldwide, according to its website, while Inditex claims 120,000, 80% female, & an average employee age of 26.(3)
Excuse me, do you work here?
She works here.
I'm looking for like, a dress. Cute. With sleeves?
We just got a few of those in new today. Let me show you.
Meet Ali. She also works here.
Employees at major fast fashion stores sign non-disclosure & non-disparagement agreements that disallow them from speaking on the record to reporters of any kind. She doesn't really look like this.
Ali, do you like your job?
I make over minimum wage.
H&M sales associates posting wages to Glassdoor.com make between $8 and $13 an hour. In Chicago, minimum wage is $8.25 per hour, but living wage is $10.48 an hour.
You must get great discounts.
um.. 10%
Health insurance?
...
How long have you been here?
At this store? Eight months. I was at a different store before that, but I transferred.
Why?

Inditex has been opening an average of 500 new stores per year around the world for the past three years; and in the US, the retail sector offered one of the only growing job markets in the last quarter.

The AC kept breaking, and I fainted a couple of times. It's pretty hard work. You're like, running back and forth with clothes all day long. You really need AC.

And then the customers... They get mad if they come in and something's not here anymore. And they always want you to tell them how good they look.

Oh. Emotional labor.

Yeah!

And you have to look good every day, and flirt with customers.

You know some workers at New York H&Ms have been joining unions?

H&M management recently expressed public support for employee unionization, although no other fast fashion retailers have followed suit.

I heard about that. But you get labelled a troublemaker if you mention it here. And this is my job.

You been doing this a long time?

Sure.

It was easier before, when we had only four or six lines a year. Then it was fun. Now it's like... There's not even room to move in here.

Inditex doubled the number of new products it offered annually to 20,000 in 2005, according to Stephanie O. Crofton High Point University Luis G Dopico Macrometrix, "Zara-Inditex and the Growth of Fast Fashion," Essays in Economic Business History, 2007. Zara now processes one million garments per day, and Forever 21 orders 100 million per year. (Cline, Overdressed)

People come in twice a week, the same people. And we're moving ten times the amount of stuff around!

Like, selling it?

Not even. Mostly it just gets shipped back to I-dont-know-where.

The NYT reported in 2010 that whole bags filled with unworn items, slashed to prevent use, were being discarded behind an H&M in Manhattan. (Jim Dwyer, "A Clothing Clearance Where More than Just the Prices Have Been Slashed," January 5), and the EPA claims 10 pounds of clothes per US citizen are discarded annually, while donations to Goodwill increased by nearly 70% in the last decade, most in clothing.

So if the clothes aren't even selling, what is fast fashion about?

It's like its own marketing strategy.

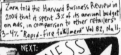

You don't see a lot of ads for the stores, just shopping bags. And if you don't come in every week you might miss something. It probably saves a ton of money.

Zara told the Harvard Business Review in 2004 that it spent .3% of its annual budget on ads, in comparison to other retailers' 3-4%. "Rapid-Fire Fulfillment" Vol 82, No 11.

Thanks, Ali.

NEXT: the BUSINESS of THRIFT

the BUSINESS of THRIFT

drawn by
Julia Gfrörer

written by
Anne Elizabeth Moore

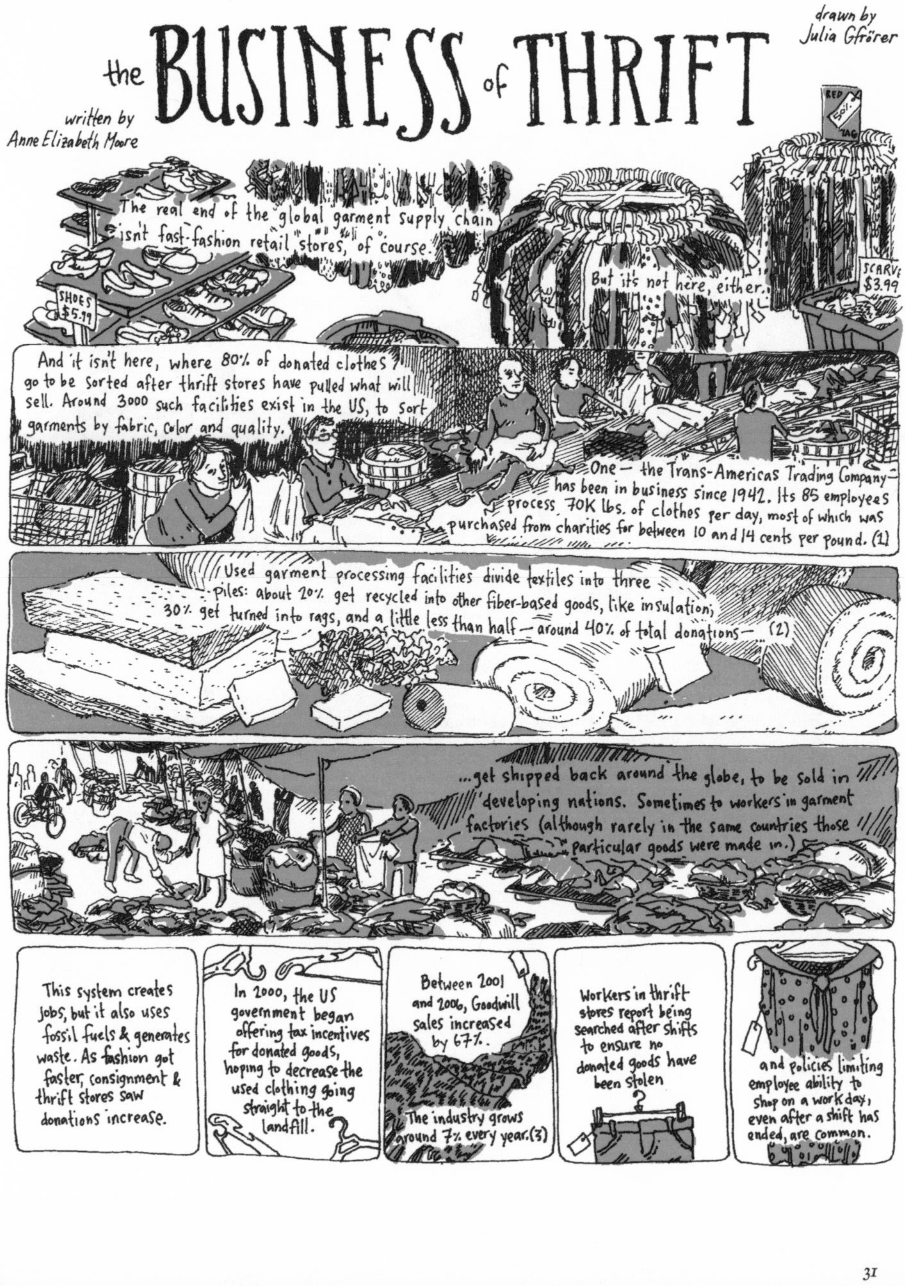
The real end of the global garment supply chain isn't fast-fashion retail stores, of course.
SHOES $5.99
But it's not here, either.
SCARVE $3.99
And it isn't here, where 80% of donated clothes go to be sorted after thrift stores have pulled what will sell. Around 3000 such facilities exist in the US, to sort garments by fabric, color and quality.
One — the Trans-Americas Trading Company — has been in business since 1942. Its 85 employees process 70K lbs. of clothes per day, most of which was purchased from charities for between 10 and 14 cents per pound. (1)
Used garment processing facilities divide textiles into three piles: about 20% get recycled into other fiber-based goods, like insulation; 30% get turned into rags, and a little less than half — around 40% of total donations — (2)
...get shipped back around the globe, to be sold in developing nations. Sometimes to workers in garment factories (although rarely in the same countries those particular goods were made in.)
This system creates jobs, but it also uses fossil fuels & generates waste. As fashion got faster, consignment & thrift stores saw donations increase.
In 2000, the US government began offering tax incentives for donated goods, hoping to decrease the used clothing going straight to the landfill.
Between 2001 and 2006, Goodwill sales increased by 67%.
The industry grows around 7% every year. (3)
Workers in thrift stores report being searched after shifts to ensure no donated goods have been stolen
and policies limiting employee ability to shop on a work day, even after a shift has ended, are common.

At not-for-profit resale shops, some employees may be unpaid volunteers.

Employees recently accused Goodwill of exploiting a Fair Labor Standards provision to pay disabled workers— around 7% of its workforce — less than minimum wage.

Thrift is big money for some.

In 2011, the 165 independent community based Goodwill organizations (some operate several stores) made a total of $4 billion. (5)

CEOs of regional Goodwills bring home an average $325K salary annually, and regional organizations can get between $8 and $11 million in taxpayer support every year. (6)

(The Salvation Army is not required to make financial statements public; St. Vincent de Paul organizations, not-for-profits structured like Goodwill, pull in between $1 to $10 million from sales every year, & between $0 and $6 million in government grants.

Then there are for-profit thrift stores, like Unique, Savers, and Value Village.

They have agreements with not-for-profit agencies that allow them to take donations and pay reduced mail rates, but are for-profit enterprises.

A fraction of earnings go back to contracted charities, but from these, fees are subtracted.

In the end, only about a quarter of the funds or less go to not-for-profit agencies. (7)

Apogee, owners of Unique Thrift stores, have been known to consistently contest unemployment claims, and fail to comply with the Americans With Disabilities Act. Workers have also accused managers at the Minnesota-based chain of sexual harassment. (8)

(There's more to the story. Americans donate about 12 lbs of garments per year to charity, but in 2012 they threw away about 70 lbs of garments each— a big increase from 2006, when each person discarded only about 10 lbs. of garments every year. (1) Used clothing makes up over 5% of all new municipal solid waste every year. (9)

The number is growing. In 1999, 18.2 million lbs of post-consumer textile waste was generated. In 2009 it was 25.46 billion lbs. And by 2019 it's predicted to hit 35.4 billion. (1) But while the throwaways increase by close to 40% every decade, recycling only increases by 2%. (9) Last year, several municipal areas even began curbside textile recycling pickup programs. (10)

ZONED

WRITTEN BY
ANNE ELIZABETH
MOORE

DRAWN BY
MELISSA MENDES

BEFORE YOUR CLOTHES GET RECYCLED, DUMPED IN THE LANDFILL, OR EVEN PURCHASED—AT THE THRIFT STORE OR THE MALL—THEY'RE PACKED UP AT WAREHOUSES AND BROUGHT IN OVERLAND BY TRUCKS.

THEY APPEAR UNREMARKABLE, BUT THESE WAREHOUSES OFTEN SIT ON LAND DENATIONALIZED FROM THE UNITED STATES AND CLASSIFIED A FOREIGN-TRADE ZONE (FTZ).

FTZ

WRITER DARA ORENSTEIN CALLS FTZs A "DECEPTIVELY SIMPLE LEGAL FICTION" THAT ALLOWS MULTINATIONAL CORPORATIONS SPACE TO ASSEMBLE OR MANUFACTURE IMPORTED GOODS WITHOUT ACCRUING THE USUAL TAXES AND TARIFFS. (1)

THERE ARE AROUND 260 FTZs IN ALL 50 STATES (PLUS 3 IN PUERTO RICO) — WITH SEVERAL NON-CONTIGUOUS SUBZONES EACH — ALTHOUGH NOT ALL ARE OPERATIONAL EVERY YEAR.

LAST YEAR'S FOREIGN-TRADE ZONE BOARD REPORTED THAT FTZs TOOK IN OVER $732 Bil IN SHIPMENTS IN 2012, AN INCREASE OVER 2011'S $640 Bil (2) — OR 35.5% OF THE 2011 US MANUFACTURING GDP, AND 4.4% OF THE TOTAL US GDP. (3)

THAT'S A LOT OF LAND — AND A LOT OF MONEY. AS ORENSTEIN POINTS OUT, FTZs ARE SPACES FOR "FRICTIONLESS PRODUCTION" WHERE THE MECHANICS OF GLOBAL TRADE CAN OPERATE SMOOTHLY...

CITY OF NEW YORK
DEPARTMENT OF DOCKS

THE UNITED STATES FIRST
FOREIGN TRADE ZONE
STATEN ISLAND, CITY OF NEW YORK
OPENED FEBRUARY 1, 1937
CITY OF NEW YORK
DEPARTMENT OF DOCKS

FOR
STATEN I
OPEN
FH LA
MAYO

... ALTHOUGH EVER SINCE THE FOREIGN-TRADE ZONES ACT OF 1934 PASSED, "FRICTION" HAS ALWAYS SORT OF MEANT "PEOPLE". (1)

A DOCUMENT UNEARTHED LAST YEAR LISTED EVIDENCE OF INEFFECTIVE AND DANGEROUS EQUIPMENT WORKERS SAY WAS NEVER FIXED, INCLUDING

↑ BAD SPARK PLUGS

BROKEN RAMPS (6) ↓

←POTENTIALLY DEADLY IF WORKERS ARE CARRYING LARGE LOADS (ALTHOUGH INSURANCE PROTECTS WAREHOUSE OWNERS FROM LIABILITY).

IT'S EASY TO MONITOR WORKERS, SINCE THE DENATIONALIZED ZONE DESIGNATION MEANS EXTENSIVE SECURITY IS A GIVEN.

SINCE SEPTEMBER 11, 2001, CONCERNS ABOUT SECURITY AND INTERNATIONAL BORDERS HAVE LED TO A BOOM IN FTZ USE, WHICH ITSELF HAS LED TO AN EMPLOYMENT BOOM, ALTHOUGH MOST JOBS ARE TEMPORARY. WORKERS AT FTZ #22 SAY 7 DIFFERENT TEMP AGENCIES MANAGE EMPLOYEES ON SITE.

THE NUMBER OF WORKERS AT FTZs IS RISING — 330,000 IN 2008 (1) TO 370,000 IN 2012 (2) — BUT THOSE NUMBERS DON'T ACCOUNT FOR INCREASING NUMBERS OF TEMPORARY EMPLOYEES.

IT'S A MOSTLY UNION-FREE LABOR FORCE. THE SECURITY AND SURVEILLANCE MEASURES AT FTZs MAKE IT HARD FOR ORGANIZERS TO GET TO WORKERS, OR FOR WORKERS TO TALK ABOUT UNIONS WITHOUT RETRIBUTION.

LAST YEAR, 13 TRUCKERS FOR PRATT INDUSTRIES IN LOWER MACUNGIE, PA (FTZ #272), COMPLAINED TO THE NATIONAL LABOR RELATIONS BOARD THAT THEIR SUDDEN TERMINATION WAS BECAUSE THEY'D BEEN PLANNING TO UNIONIZE. (4)

IN JUNE, FOREVER 21 WAREHOUSE WORKERS NEAR LA, CA INITIATED A CLASS-ACTION LAWSUIT ALLEGING THEY WEREN'T PROVIDED AMPLE MEALTIMES, BREAKS, OR OVERTIME COMPENSATION. (5)

INSIDE THE WALMART WAREHOUSE IN JOLIET, IL, (FTZ #22) - THE LARGEST AND BUSIEST FTZ IN THE COUNTRY - WORKERS TELL US THAT TEMPERATURES GET TO BE AS HIGH AS 120°F IN THE SUMMER AND AS LOW AS 0° IN THE WINTER. FEMALE EMPLOYEES HAVE BEEN SUBJECTED TO SEXUAL ASSAULT AND UNPREDICTABLE HOURS.

We're supposed to get two 10 minute breaks per day, but that doesn't even give us time to get to the exit.

Bag searches before and after lunch eat up our whole 30-minute meal break.

THE PRACTICE OF LOCKING WORKERS IN DURING SHIFTS MEANS WORKERS WITH CHILDREN AT HOME MUST HAVE SAFE, RELIABLE CHILDCARE - HARD TO FIND ON $10 AN HOUR, ESPECIALLY SINCE THERE'S NO COMPENSATION FOR TRAVEL. FTZs ARE OFTEN ONLY ACCESSIBLE BY CAR AND FAR FROM URBAN CENTERS.

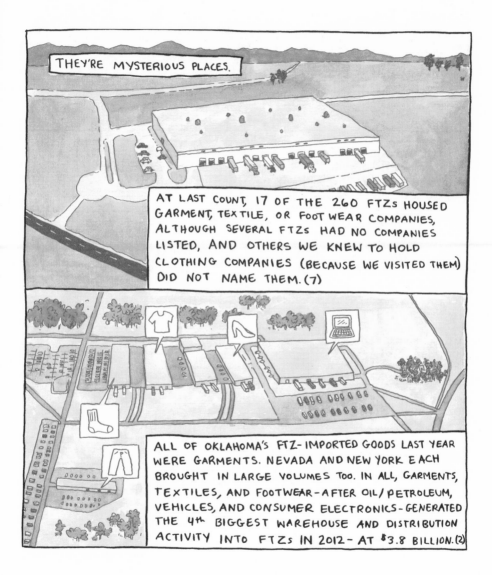

THEY'RE MYSTERIOUS PLACES.

AT LAST COUNT, 17 OF THE 260 FTZs HOUSED GARMENT, TEXTILE, OR FOOTWEAR COMPANIES, ALTHOUGH SEVERAL FTZs HAD NO COMPANIES LISTED, AND OTHERS WE KNEW TO HOLD CLOTHING COMPANIES (BECAUSE WE VISITED THEM) DID NOT NAME THEM. (7)

ALL OF OKLAHOMA'S FTZ-IMPORTED GOODS LAST YEAR WERE GARMENTS. NEVADA AND NEW YORK EACH BROUGHT IN LARGE VOLUMES TOO. IN ALL, GARMENTS, TEXTILES, AND FOOTWEAR-AFTER OIL/PETROLEUM, VEHICLES, AND CONSUMER ELECTRONICS-GENERATED THE 4th BIGGEST WAREHOUSE AND DISTRIBUTION ACTIVITY INTO FTZs IN 2012 - AT $3.8 BILLION. (2)

RED TAPE

THE BACKBONE OF THE GLOBAL GARMENT INDUSTRY IS THE VAST NETWORK OF INTERNATIONAL TRADE AGREEMENTS THAT DICTATE WHO WILL IMPORT WHAT TO SELL WHERE, AND UNDER WHAT CONDITIONS—

OFTEN AGREEMENTS THUNK UP RIGHT HERE IN LI'L OLE 'MERICA.

IT'S IRONIC, CONSIDERING HOW DEEPLY COTTON PRODUCTION IS WOVEN INTO THE FABRIC OF US HISTORY, BUT ONE UPSHOT OF THESE DEALS HAS BEEN TO OUTSOURCE JOBS THAT, AT VARIOUS POINTS, DEFINED AMERICAN LAND, LIFE, AND LIBERTY.

WRITTEN BY
ANNE ELIZABETH
MOORE
DRAWN BY
MELISSA MENDES

BEFORE THE NORTH AMERICAN FREE TRADE AGREEMENT (NAFTA)
TOOK EFFECT IN 1994, SOME 49,100 APPAREL JOBS WERE LOST
(A LITTLE OVER 5% OF THE TOTAL) OVER 4 YEARS.

¿Es hora de dejar de fumar todavía?

Deseo.

BETWEEN 1995 AND 2007, HOWEVER—
FROM NAFTA TO SHORTLY BEFORE
THE ECONOMIC COLLAPSE OF 2008—
US APPAREL JOBS LARGELY
VANISHED: 629,000, NEARLY 74%.

DURING THE SAME TIME PERIOD, DEMAND
WENT UP BY ABOUT 80%. (1) ECONOMIST
PIETRA RIVOLI NOTES THAT HALF THE
JOBS IN THE US GARMENT INDUSTRY
DISAPPEARED BETWEEN 2000 AND 2007.

IT'S AFFECTED TRADE ORGANIZATIONS TOO.
ONCE-VENERATED INSTITUTIONS LIKE

THE
NATIONAL

THE
AMERICAN
SWEATER ASSOCIATION

HEAVY OUTERWEAR
ASSOCIATION

THE
TROUSER
INSTITUTE of
AMERICA

NO LONGER EXIST, HAVING LITTLE
DOMESTIC TRADE TO PROTECT.

THESE AGREEMENTS DICTATE EVERY MOVE YOUR CLOTHES MAKE BEFORE THEY GET TO A FOREIGN-TRADE ZONE—EACH STEP CAREFULLY OUTLINED, IN ADVANCE, BY US CONGRESS AND RELEVANT HEADS OF STATE.

安静

IT'S GENDERED, OF COURSE: AN 82% MALE GROUP OF LAWMAKERS SET RULES PERTAINING TO THE LIVELIHOODS OF ABOUT 50 MILLION WOMEN IN THE GARMENT INDUSTRY WORLDWIDE.

IN FACT, RIVOLI WRITES, "THE TEXTILE AND APPAREL TRADE IS THE MOST MANAGED AND PROTECTED TRADE IN US HISTORY." (2)

APPAREL UPDATE

APPAREL UPDATE

WHAT THAT MEANS, REALLY, IS THAT THE GARMENT TRADE IS MADE UP OF AN UNBELIEVABLY COMPLEX SET OF RULES THAT CHANGE SO FREQUENTLY MOST IN THE INDUSTRY CAN'T KEEP UP. (3)

THE RULES ARE VERY DETAILED. THEY DON'T JUST COVER, LIKE, BRAS—

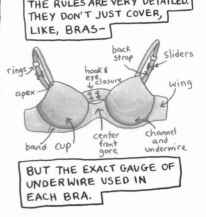

back strap
sliders
rings
hook & eye closure
apex
wing
band cup
center front gore
channel and underwire

BUT THE EXACT GAUGE OF UNDERWIRE USED IN EACH BRA.

US CONGRESSWOMAN MARCY KAPTUR (D-OH) THOUGHT IT ALL SMELLED FISHY BY THE TIME THE DOMINICAN REPUBLIC AND CENTRAL AMERICAN FREE TRADE AGREEMENT (DR-CAFTA) CAME UP FOR A VOTE IN 2005.

"[It] will become another job-killing trade agreement the American people don't want. (4)

IT PASSED BY ONLY A NARROW MARGIN-217-215.

(IT'S HIS JOB TO CHECK THE GAUGE OF THAT WIRE.)

YUP, THIS MAKES THE UNDERWIRE IN YOUR BRA A SECURITY ISSUE.

MORE CORRECTLY STATED, U.S. CUSTOMS AND BORDER PROTECTION (CBP)-A COMPONENT OF THE DEPARTMENT OF HOMELAND SECURITY (DHS)-HAS DESIGNATED TEXTILE AND APPAREL AGREEMENTS A PRIORITY TRADE ISSUE (PTI).

We've got a .7mm gauge on this one.

"THE GOAL OF THE TEXTILES PTI IS TO ENSURE THAT TEXTILE IMPORTS, WHICH GENERATE MORE THAN 40% OF THE DUTIES COLLECTED BY CBP, FULLY COMPLY WITH APPLICABLE LAWS, REGULATIONS, QUOTAS, FREE TRADE AGREEMENT REQUIREMENTS, AND INTELLECTUAL PROPERTY PROVISIONS." (5)

STILL CONFUSED? LET THESE COMMITTEE ON HOMELAND SECURITY REMARKS FROM 2009 SORT IT OUT FOR YOU.

That is what homeland security intelligence is all about: getting accurate, actionable, and timely information to the officers in our hometowns so they know who and what to look for in order to prevent the next 9/11... if homeland security intelligence is done the right way, countless lives can be saved.

HON. REP. JANE HARMAN

JOHN W. GAISSERT

Our domestic counterterrorism doctrine has not fully addressed the evolution of terrorist strategies... They are fighting us using financial crime to counterfeit clothing, pirate CD's, DVD's, sunglasses, and other articles, perpetrate related fraud and the criminal laundering of money.

KEEP IN MIND: THE FASHION INDUSTRY EMPLOYS ONE IN SEVEN WOMEN WORLDWIDE, MOST IN DEVELOPING NATIONS. THAT'S A LOT OF TERRORISTS!

Endnotes for Chapter One

Fast Fashion

1. "100 Years of consumer spending," U.S. Department of Labor, Bureau of Labor Statistics, May 2006. http://www.bls.gov/opub/uscs/report991.pdf (Accessed April 26, 2015).

2. Inditex, the Spanish forerunner of fast fashion stores, had an incredible year in 2005, immediately following the expiration of the Multi-Fibre Agreement of 1974. Stephanie O. Crofton and Luis G. Dopico. "Zara-Inditex and the growth of Fast Fashion," *Essays in Economic and Business History*, Vol XXV, 2007.

Model Employee

1. Unless otherwise attributed, all Sarah Meier's quotes come from a videochat interview with Anne Elizabeth Moore recorded on November 13, 2014.

2. "How I met Sarah Meier," *How I Met (Your Brand)*, June 24, 2013. http://himyb.com/2013/06/24/how-i-met-sarah-meier/ (accessed February 9, 2015).

3. "Industry Analysis," Model Alliance, 2012. http://modelalliance.org/industry-analysis (accessed February 9, 2015).

4. Sara Ziff. "Yes, you should feel bad for models," *The Guardian*, September 9, 2014. http://www.theguardian.com/commentisfree/2014/sep/09/models-diet-go-broke-modeling-industry (accessed September 14, 2015).

5. Kate Dries. "New York Fashion Week," *Jezebel*, February 14, 2014. http://jezebel.com/new-york-fashion-week-diversity-talks-but-white-faces-1522416724 (accessed February 9, 2015).

6. "Industry Analysis," Ibid.

7. Ibid.

8. Ibid.

9. Ibid.

10. Ibid.

11. "Women and work in the garment industry," ILO Better Factories Cambodia and the World Bank, December 2006, http://siteresources.worldbank.org/INTJUSFORPOOR/

Resources/WomenandWorkinthefactory.pdf (accessed February 9, 2015) and "Action oriented research on gender equality and the working and living conditions of garment factory workers in Cambodia," International Labour Organization, 2012, http://www.ilo. org/wcmsp5/groups/public/~asia/~ro-bangkok/~sro-bangkok/documents/publication/ wcms_204166.pdf (accessed February 9, 2015).

12. "Occupational Employment and Wages: Models," U.S. Department of Labor, Bureau of Labor Statistics, May 2013. http://www.bls.gov/oes/current/oes419012.htm (accessed February 9, 2015).

13. Living Wage Calculator. http://livingwage.mit.edu/states/36 (accessed February 9, 2015).

Let's Go Shopping

1. Elizabeth Cline, "Fashion Fast Facts," *Overdressed* The Book website. http://www. overdressedthebook.com/fashion-fast-facts/ (accessed September 14, 2015).

2. Mango alone claims 11,200 employees worldwide, 1800 of whom work at the design center at Mango HQ. Employees average, the website states, 32 years of age and are 82% female. (See company website: http://shop.mango.com/home.faces?state=she_400_US, accessed February 9, 2015.) H&M has 104,000 employees worldwide, according to its website, while Inditex claims 120,000, 80% female, and an average employee age of 26. (Company website again: http://www.inditex.com/en/who_we_are/our_team, accessed February 9, 2014.)

Business of Thrift

1. Pietra Rizoli, *The Travels of a T-Shirt in the Global Economy*, Wiley (Hoboken NJ, 2009), pg. 219.

2. The Council for Textile Recycling website, http://www.weardonaterecycle.org (accessed September 14, 2015).

3. "Industry Statistics and Trends," National Association of Resale and Thrift Shops, http:// www.narts.org (accessed September 14, 2015).

4. See the petition "Goodwill Industries International: Pay Disabled Workers a Real Wage," at Change.org/Goodwill (accessed September 14, 2015).

5. "About Us," Goodwill website. http://www.goodwill.org/about-us/ (accessed September 14, 2015).

6. "Goodwill's charity racket," John Rhabe, *Huffington Post*, September 25, 2012. http://www.huffingtonpost.com/john-hrabe/the-worst-corporation-in-_b_1876905.html (accessed August 1, 2013).

7. "For profit thrift stores attract a growing following in NJ, but some question chain's methods," *New Jersey Star-Ledger*, August 29, 2010. http://www.nj.com/news/index.ssf/2010/08/unique_thrift_stores_are_newes.html (accessed August 1, 2013).

8. See numerous claims made at Apogee Retail Watch, http://apogeeretailwatch.blogspot.com (accessed September 14, 2015).

9. "Municipal Solid Waste in the United States," U.S. Environmental Protection Agency Office of Solid Waste, December 2010. http://www.epa.gov/wastes/nonhaz/municipal/pubs/msw2009rpt.pdf (accessed September 14, 2015).

10. "Clothing Recycling Goes Curbside as Demand Rises," Wendy Koch, *USA Today*, April 24, 2013. http://www.usatoday.com/story/news/nation/2013/04/20/recyling-clothes-expands-curbside/2092351/ (accessed September 14, 2015).

Zoned

1. Dara Orenstein, "Foreign-trade zones and the cultural logic of frictionless production," *Radical History Review*, Winter 2011.

2. See the Foreign-Trade Zone Board Annual Reports to Congress at http://ia.ita.doc.gov/ftzpage/annual-report.html (accessed September 14, 2015).

3. "US Manufacturing in Context," Manufacturing.gov. http://www.manufacturing.gov/mfg_in_context.html#_ftn1 (accessed September 14, 2015).

4. Spencer Soper. "Truck drivers claim union talk cost them their jobs," *The Morning Call*, May 19, 2012. http://articles.mcall.com/2012-05-19/business/mc-pratt-union-complaint-20120519_1_truck-drivers-union-avoidance-consultants-vote-for-union-representation (accessed September 14, 2015).

5. Khorrami Boucher. "Forever 21 face class action lawsuit," *Fair Employment Legal Update*: http://fairemploymentlegalupdate.com/2013/06/10/forever-21-faces-class-action-lawsuit/ (accessed September 14, 2015).

6. "Supervisor Dock Check Sheet," *Caught! Secret Walmart warehouse document revealed*, Warehouse Workers United website. http://www.warehouseworkersunited.org/caught-secret-walmart-warehouse-document-revealed/ (accessed September 14, 2015).

7. "FTZ Map," International Trade Administration of the Department of Commerce. http://ia.ita.doc.gov/ftzpage/letters/ftzlist-map.html (accessed February 18, 2016).

Red Tape

1. See the American Manufacturing Trade Action Coalition citing the Bureau of Labor Statistics report at mbginfovcs.com.

2. Pietra Rizoli, *The Travels of a T-Shirt in the Global Economy*, Wiley (Hoboken NJ, 2009).

3. The existence of these prohibitions is often used to explain why so-called free-trade agreements don't work, although these arguments overlook the human and labor rights issues that happen in the absence of such restrictions.

4. Jim Abrams, "U.S. House approves CAFTA," *La Prensa*, August 2, 2005. http://www.laprensatoledo.com/Stories/2005/Aug%203%202005/U.S.%20House%20approves%20CAFTA.htm (accessed September 14, 2015).

5. "Priority Trade Issues: Textiles," U.S. Customs and Border Patrol website. http://www.cbp.gov/xp/cgov/home.xml (accessed September 14, 2015).

6. As "Homeland Security Intelligence: Its Relevance and Limitations," Hearing before the Subcommittee on Intelligence, Information Sharing, and Risk Assessment, Department of Homeland Security, (Washington DC, March 18 2009). http://www.fas.org/irp/congress/2009_hr/hsin.html (accessed September 14, 2015).

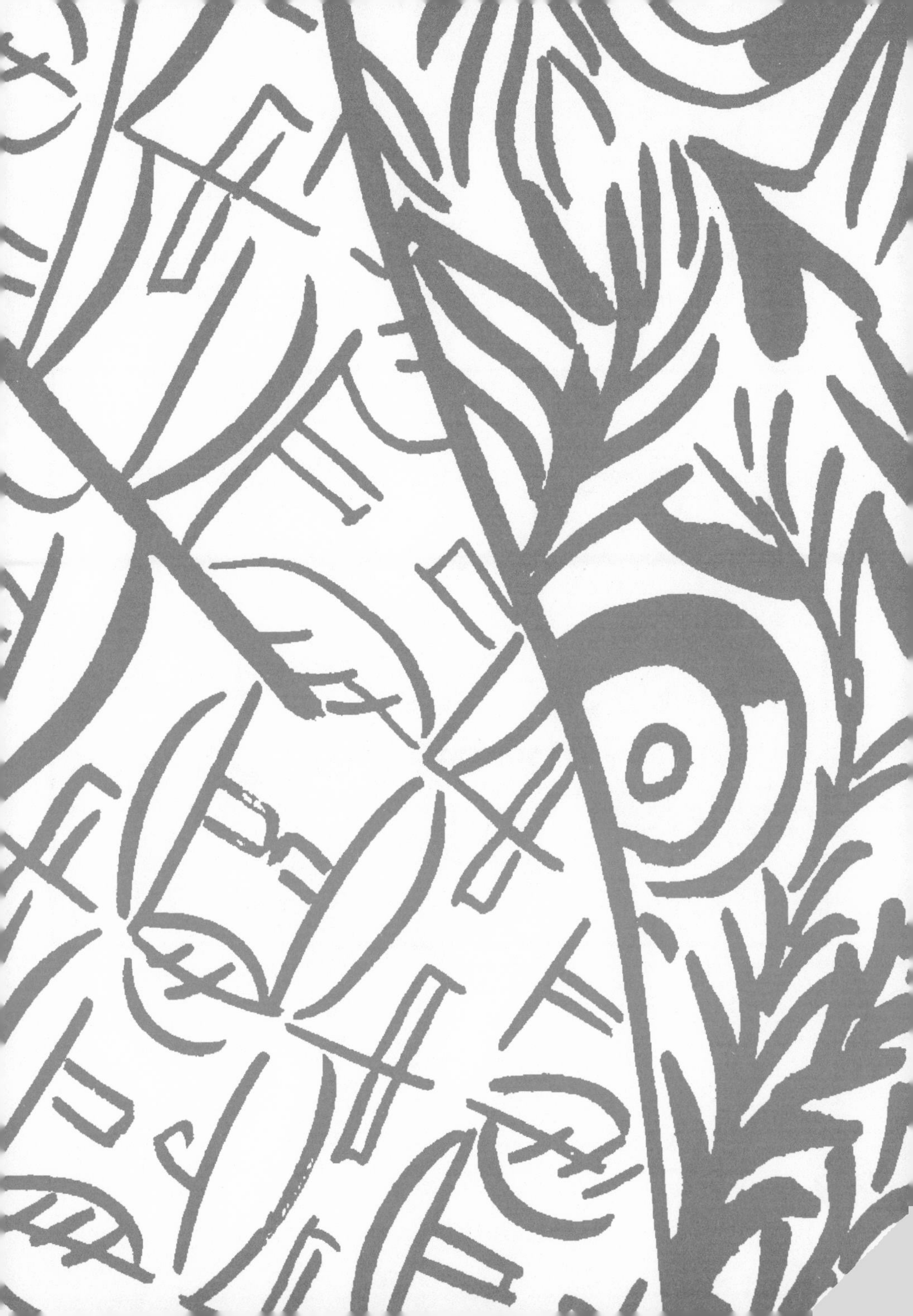

Chapter 2 : Austria

In my young adulthood, I was enamored of men's fashion in Austria: Waldveirtlers, for example, offered a classic, high-quality leather boot that somehow exuded a casual, androgynous cool in direct negation of my own aggressively cool Doc Martens. I perceived a near-French adoration of scarves. Skinny but not skin-tight jeans. Simple cotton ring-necked shirts dyed in natural tones like wine or forest, if not black. No one bathed; it was the 1990s. We didn't bathe in the U.S. either. On visits, I would import American peanut butters and toothpastes for my friends. After every trip, I brought home suitcases full of pumpkin seed oil and Styrian wine.

My interest in men's fashion gradually waned. In the fall of 2013, I realized there was a reason. I was sitting in a bar in the capital city, Vienna—and even the bar was different. Airy, not dark and wooden. No local or even German indie music playing, but some overproduced electronic international dance thing. The wine list had wines from around the world, and my friend and I drank something French. This was my first clue: I was in the country that produced several of my favorite wines in the world. I looked around and was not aesthetically impressed by the dress of our fellow patrons. "What happened to men's fashion?" I asked my companion. The table to our right was filled with men who spoke English to each other in Austrian accents. They wore standard, dark-colored business suits and spoke of their common workplace, a bank. "When did it get so boring?"

It wasn't just fashion, of course, and certainly not just men's apparel. Nowadays, the American toothpastes and peanut butters of my youth are produced under their original American brand names in factories just outside of Vienna and sold at local drug stores throughout the country; it's easier to get pumpkin seed oil in the U.S. than it used to be, although it is not yet mass produced here (a rare instance of globalization that I would applaud). Even less corporate-backed food trends jump the pond quickly: When I was researching these strips in Vienna in May 2014, I could not find kale anywhere, although it was mentioned on the cover of nearly every magazine in the airport when I left the U.S. Five months later, when I returned to present the completed strips at Vienna Art Week, kale had arrived. It was available in every grocery store, as if it had always been there.

The shifts in fashion over the years had garnered a similar lack of attention. Few I spoke to could pinpoint that any change had occurred at all. I'd originally intended the Austrian chapter of this book to be composed of interviews with men recalling how and when they'd undertaken changes in dress and style. Some of this remains—my interview with Simon Häussle, who I later asked to draw a few strips for the book, offers insight into how individuals adopt the uniform of the global citizen—but the larger picture that was building quickly captured the majority of my attention. Austria had been a proud textile-producing nation, deeply invested in local production and hand-crafted wares. A vast political agenda had been enacted to uproot those instincts—a force we now call neoliberalism—and folks like Johann Perzi (page 62) are feeling the change personally. Remnants of earlier days are present, certainly—"Connie, Urban Planner," (page 72) who comes from a textile-producing family, notes the recent reprise of the dirndl and the spectacle of Conchita Wurst—but as Connie explains, tiny nods to individual choice hide within them a cultural conservativism that may not have Austria's best interests at heart. I remain intrigued by how few noticed the massive cultural shifts, but the larger story—of who initiated these changes, and how folks brought them about—eventually took over the chapter.

While many of these strips were first published in a limited, two-color risograph edition printed by the good people at Issue Press in Grand Rapids, Michigan—including several shorter strips not included here—Delia Jean's opening strip, "Die Arbeitslosen von Marienthal," appears here for the first time. None have been published digitally; all were created in residency at das weisse haus in Vienna, Austria, and published with their support.

DIE ARBEITSLOSEN von Marienthal

In 1930, three researchers from the Institute of Psychology at the University of Austria—Marie Jahoda, Paul F. Lazarsfeld, and Hans Zeisel—began a project to study the effects of unemployment. Popular opinion at the time held that job loss led to revolution, but these researchers suspected instead what we know to be true today.

"Prolonged unemployment leads to a state of apathy in which the victims do not utilize any longer even the few opportunities left to them." (1)

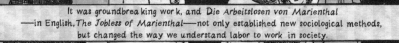

It was groundbreaking work, and *Die Arbeitslosen von Marienthal* —in English, *The Jobless of Marienthal*—not only established new sociological methods, but changed the way we understand labor to work in society.

It's not as if Austria—or even the capital, Vienna—is known today as a fashion center. It's also not known as a garment-producing nation. Today it's more a place where clothes from elsewhere are consumed.

It wasn't always this way.

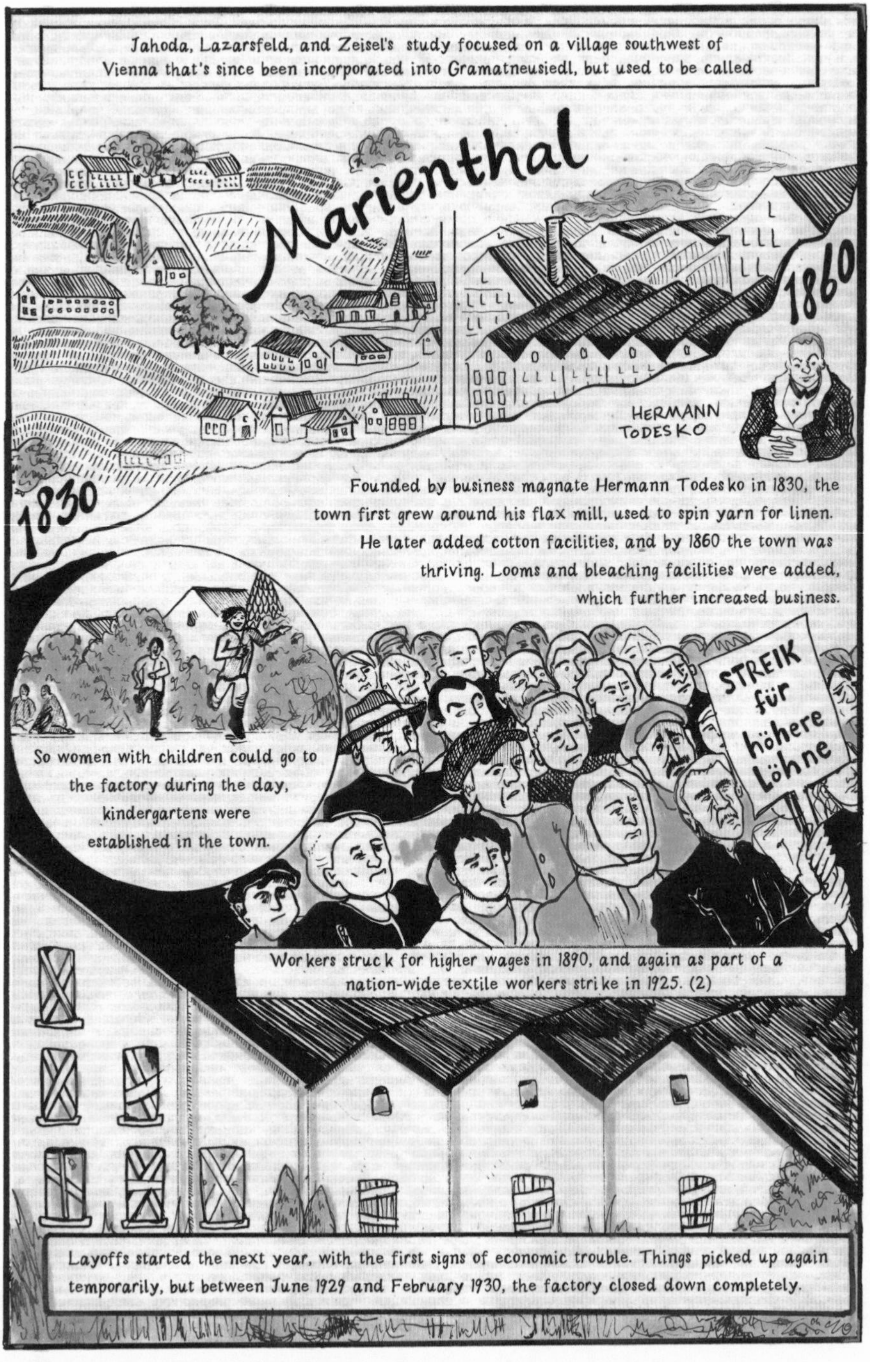

Jahoda, Lazarsfeld, and Zeisel's study focused on a village southwest of Vienna that's since been incorporated into Gramatneusiedl, but used to be called
Marienthal
1830
1860
HERMANN TODESKO
Founded by business magnate Hermann Todesko in 1830, the town first grew around his flax mill, used to spin yarn for linen. He later added cotton facilities, and by 1860 the town was thriving. Looms and bleaching facilities were added, which further increased business.
So women with children could go to the factory during the day, kindergartens were established in the town.
STREIK für höhere Löhne
Workers struck for higher wages in 1890, and again as part of a nation-wide textile workers strike in 1925. (2)
Layoffs started the next year, with the first signs of economic trouble. Things picked up again temporarily, but between June 1929 and February 1930, the factory closed down completely.

By early 1930, the entire population of 1486 people (49% male, 51% female) was completely out of work. (3) Austria's response to mass employment was the dole, a system that offered unemployment compensation as long as no work of any kind for payment was performed.

The enforced idleness, on top of poverty, caused "a depression that was much worse than anything the United States went through." (4)

The very way individuals participate in society had ceased to function.

Marienthal residents no longer felt productive. Even the number of books checked out of the library—a free public service—declined from about 3 and a half books per reader in 1929 to one and a half in 1931. (5)

"It is quite probable that part of the success of the early Hitler movement came about because large numbers of unemployed were taken into barracks and kept busy," (6)

Lazarsfeld wrote in the introduction to the American edition of their book.

The authors note, but don't look too closely at, how the "idleness" of mass unemployment was also gendered: in Marienthal, men tended to give up trips to Vienna or the pub or newspapers; women maintained the health and well-being of the children and mended the family's clothing. (7)

The end result is that women averaged an hour and a half less sleep per night than men. (8)

For men,

the pace of life
changed substantially
—slowed.

Only 8% of the men
in the village
walked to their
destinations
without stopping.

Nearly a quarter
stopped once, while
more than half
stopped three
or more times. (9)

(Compare to
the women
in the village—
the majority of
whom were too busy
to leave the house.
Of those that did,
84% stopped once
or not at all.)

"For every 100 persons
walking in the
street, there were
always about 30
standing around," the
authors note.
"The average speed
of movement was
extremely low." (10)

"Even the officials no longer pretend that it is possible to live on relief money," the authors wrote. "When the farmers find that cabbages and potatoes are disappearing from their fields, they hardly ever take action." (12)

While some in the town maintained good spirits and others fell into despair, food and entertainment could still be found in occasional, if minimal, supply. Other necessities were less easy to come by.

For residents of a village built around a textile factory, it is ironic that one of the most significant causes for concern was apparel.

"There is no allowance for [the] replacement [of clothes] or even for their repair in the carefully balanced budget of a Marienthal household. ... That wear and tear did not raise great havoc earlier is due to the fact that people had unusually large amounts of textiles, which they used to get from the factory for next to nothing." (16)

The authors wrote.

"The moment will come when shoes and clothes, repeatedly mended, finally reach the stage where they can no longer be repaired." (17)

Austria's textile industry later picked up, and then fell off again. It's the perfect place to consider how the people we don't think of as enmeshed in the global garment trade really are.

written by
ANNE ELIZABETH MOORE

drawn by
DELIA JEAN

Coming next time:
ANDREA KOMLOSY, RESEARCHER

IT'S ASTONISHING TO ME THAT YOU WOULD LOOK AT AUSTRIA. IT'S NOT SUCH A GREAT PLACE. VIENNA IS A HOT SPOT FOR FASHION, BUT AUSTRIA ...

VIENNA, AUSTRIA

AUSTRIAN TEXTILES IS ONE SPECIALTY OF MINE, BUT IT ALL BECOMES GLOBALIZED AT A CERTAIN MOMENT. ACTUALLY I FOUND THAT GLOBALIZATION IS QUITE OLD. I DO NOT SPEAK OF TRADE. ASIAN AND EUROPEAN TEXTILES AND SO ON, ARE A PART OF GLOBALIZATION ALREADY IN THE VERY EARLY TIMES. (1)

BUT ALMOST AS EARLY, YOU HAVE GLOBAL COMMODITY CHAINS, WHERE COMPANIES ARE SOURCING IN INDIA, FOR INSTANCE. MY INTEREST IS IN WHAT GLOBAL CONNECTIONS MAKE THE LOCAL POSSIBLE.

SPINNING, WEAVING, THE SOCIAL HISTORY – I KNOW IT QUITE WELL. HOW IT CHANGED FROM CRAFT TO INDUSTRY. AND GARMENTS COME IN WHEN GARMENTS BECAME PART OF THE CHAIN. FOR A LONG TIME, THE CHAIN ENDED MORE OR LESS WITH THE FABRIC AT THE TAILORS, OR GARMENTS THAT WERE MANUFACTURED AT HOME.

AUSTRIAN TEXTILES WERE QUITE ROBUST A CENTURY AND A HALF AGO. RECENTLY, NATIONAL PRODUCTION HAS FALLEN OFF DRAMATICALLY.

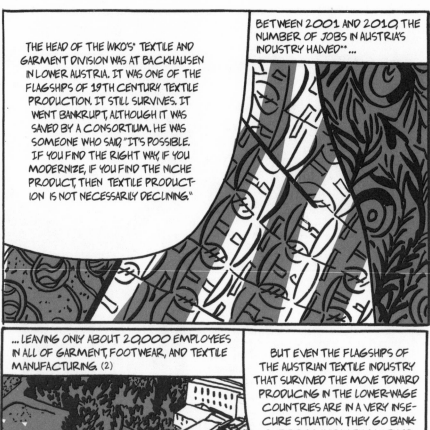

THE HEAD OF THE WKO'S* TEXTILE AND GARMENT DIVISION WAS AT BACKHAUSEN IN LOWER AUSTRIA. IT WAS ONE OF THE FLAGSHIPS OF 19TH CENTURY TEXTILE PRODUCTION. IT STILL SURVIVES. IT WENT BANKRUPT, ALTHOUGH IT WAS SAVED BY A CONSORTIUM. HE WAS SOMEONE WHO SAID, "IT'S POSSIBLE. IF YOU FIND THE RIGHT WAY, IF YOU MODERNIZE, IF YOU FIND THE NICHE PRODUCT, THEN TEXTILE PRODUCTION IS NOT NECESSARILY DECLINING."

BETWEEN 2001 AND 2010, THE NUMBER OF JOBS IN AUSTRIA'S INDUSTRY HALVED** ...

... LEAVING ONLY ABOUT 20,000 EMPLOYEES IN ALL OF GARMENT, FOOTWEAR, AND TEXTILE MANUFACTURING. (2)

BUT EVEN THE FLAGSHIPS OF THE AUSTRIAN TEXTILE INDUSTRY THAT SURVIVED THE MOVE TOWARD PRODUCING IN THE LOWER-WAGE COUNTRIES ARE IN A VERY INSECURE SITUATION. THEY GO BANKRUPT REGULARLY, THEN OTHER CONSORTIUMS TRY TO SAVE THEM, BUT IT'S A QUESTION OF TIME UNTIL THEY ARE GONE.

WRITTEN BY: ANNE ELIZABETH MOORE
DRAWN BY: SIMON HÄUSSLE

THERE ARE MAYBE HUNDREDS OF LOCALLY OWNED APPAREL OUTLETS. I'M NOT SURE HOW THEY ARE ORGANIZED, BUT I HAVE THE IMPRESSION THAT THEY MANUFACTURE OUTSIDE OF AUSTRIA.

AS I WALK THROUGH THE STREETS, I'M QUITE AWARE OF THE CHANGE. IT'S BEEN A LONG TIME SINCE YOU HAD THESE AUSTRIAN SHOPS WHICH TENDED TO BUY FROM AUSTRIAN SUPPLIERS. BUT NOW YOU HAVE INTERNATIONAL CHAINS, AND I DON'T THINK THEY HAVE AUSTRIAN SUPPLIERS, OR YOU HAVE THESE CHEAP PRODUCTS FROM TURKEY OR CHINA.

IT WAS VERY SLOW. THE OLD FAMILY-OWNED SHOPS IN TOWN HAD A CHANGE IN THEIR RENT.

THE RULE USED TO BE, IF YOU RENTED, YOU COULD NOT BE KICKED OUT, OR THE RENT COULD NOT BE RAISED, OR ONLY BY A CERTAIN AMOUNT. BUT THEN THERE WAS A NEW LAW IN THE MID-1980S OR MID-1990S THAT SAID THAT IF THERE WAS A MINOR CHANGE IN THE LEGAL FORMATION OF THE COMPANY, THEN THERE IS A NEW NEGOTIATION OF THE PRICE.

SO IF THERE WAS A SUCCESSOR IN THE FAMILY BUSINESS, THERE WAS A NEW NEGOTIATION. IF THERE WAS A NEW PARTNER, OR THE COMPANY CHANGED THAT'S QUITE NORMAL. THAT WAS NOT ONLY IN THE GARMENT TRADE, OF COURSE. BOOKSTORES DISAPPEARED LIKE THIS.

SHOPPING WAS NEVER MY FAVORITE, BUT AS A CHILD I REMEMBER GOING TO TOWN WITH MY MOTHER, AND IT WAS QUITE NICE. IN THE MIDDLE OF THE TOWN YOU HAD SHOPS WITH LOCAL SHOP OWNERS AND IT WAS QUITE CLEAR WHEN YOU CAME IN, YOU WERE WELL KNOWN. THE SHOP OWNERS ONLY HAD THIS SINGLE SHOP, OR MAYBE THEY HAD ANOTHER ONE.

VOECKLABRUCK, 1960

THERE'S A CHILDREN'S CHAIN, DOHNAL HAUS DES KINDES, AND THEY SURVIVED. BUT THAT IS RETAIL. WHERE THEY BUY AND WHAT THEY SELL, THAT IS A DIFFERENT THING. I'M NOT SURE WHAT CAME FIRST, THE DECLINE OF THE SHOPS THAT MADE IT MORE DIFFICULT FOR AUSTRIAN PRODUCERS TO HAVE THEIR PRODUCTS SOLD, OR IF THESE COMPANIES CLOSED DOWN BECAUSE THEY COULD NOT AFFORD THEIR LOCATION ANYMORE.

TO MY MIND, IT'S QUITE CLEAR THAT IT IS PART OF A CONCENTRATION PROCESS. YOU CAN SUPPORT THE CONCENTRATION PROCESS BY REGULATING IT IN A WAY THAT THE SMALLER PARTICIPANTS HAVE TO ADAPT, AND MANY ARE NOT ABLE TO DO THAT.

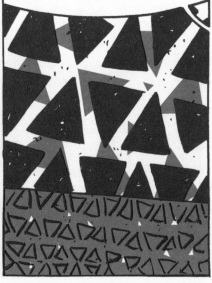

IT'S SIMILAR TO THE EUROPEAN UNION. I'M NOT IN FAVOR OF IT: I DON'T BELIEVE IN THE PEACE PROCESS AND FRIENDSHIP-MAKING AND OVERCOMING NATIONALISM AND ALL THESE THINGS. I MEAN, OF COURSE THAT WOULD BE A GOOD THING, BUT THE MAIN PURPOSE IS TO CREATE A MARKET. IT'S NOT ONLY THE EUROPEAN UNION, OF COURSE, BUT THIS INVOLVED A MAJOR LEGAL REARRANGEMENT THAT MADE IT MUCH MORE COMPLICATED FOR SMALLER FIRMS TO SURVIVE. OF COURSE SOME COULD, BUT ESPECIALLY IN CONSUMER GOODS, WHERE THERE WAS ALREADY PRESSURE FROM LOWER-WAGE COUNTRIES AND FROM CHANGING REGULATIONS, I THINK IT WAS MORE LIKE, THE END.

IN 1990, I SET UP A MUSEUM IN A FORMER TEXTILE MILL. THE MILL HAD CLOSED IN THE BEGINNING OF THE 20TH CENTURY, SO IT WAS A PROJECT THAT WAS EMBEDDED IN THE DECLINE OF THE TEXTILE INDUSTRY, WHICH WAS VERY IMPORTANT. THE MUSEUM [RELIED ON THE FACT THAT] AUSTRIA WAS A FAMOUS TEXTILE PRODUCER. IT'S [NOSTALGIA,] VERY SIMILAR TO HOW BANDS AND SINGERS GET VERY POPULAR WHO SAY, IF YOU COME TO MY CONCERT, WEAR A DIRNDL, OR A TRADITIONAL COSTUME.

THAT'S WHY I LOOK AT AUSTRIAN TEXTILE PRODUCTION AS A CHAPTER WHICH IS CLOSED.

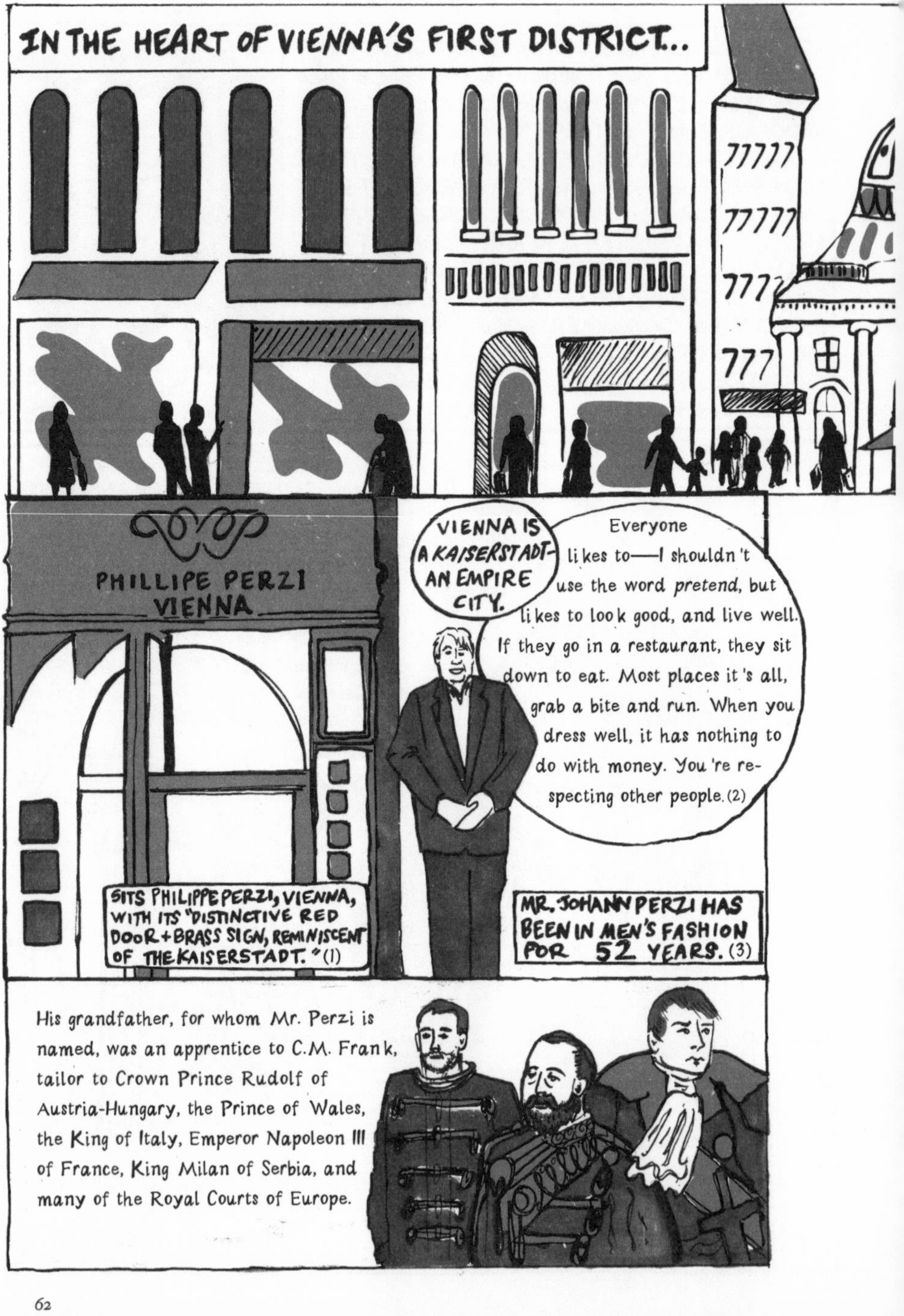
IN THE HEART OF VIENNA'S FIRST DISTRICT..
PHILLIPE PERZI VIENNA
SITS PHILIPPE PERZI, VIENNA, WITH ITS "DISTINCTIVE RED DOOR + BRASS SIGN, REMINISCENT OF THE KAISERSTADT." (1)
VIENNA IS A KAISERSTADT- AN EMPIRE CITY.
Everyone likes to—I shouldn't use the word *pretend*, but likes to look good, and live well. If they go in a restaurant, they sit down to eat. Most places it's all, grab a bite and run. When you dress well, it has nothing to do with money. You're respecting other people. (2)
MR. JOHANN PERZI HAS BEEN IN MEN'S FASHION FOR 52 YEARS. (3)
His grandfather, for whom Mr. Perzi is named, was an apprentice to C.M. Frank, tailor to Crown Prince Rudolf of Austria-Hungary, the Prince of Wales, the King of Italy, Emperor Napoleon III of France, King Milan of Serbia, and many of the Royal Courts of Europe.

JOHANN PERZI
TAILOR

We [also] had a shop in Australia. I was working for a big company in Austria, Kleider Bauer. I was the second buyer for 11 years, and I had my own shop in Australia. I was in Mauritius a couple years, producing shirts. I was in Turkey for a year. We sold shirts [as a supplier] to very, very nice people in Europe.

CARRYING ON THE TRADITION, MR. PERZI'S FATHER, PHILIPPE, OPENED THIS SHOP.

Vienna's a very strange city, in [terms of] textiles. You're losing all the tailors here now. The changes are all coming in this moment. It's very traumatic. I have my heart and soul in the menswear industry.

BUT IN AUSTRIA— AND ALL OVER EUROPE— FASHION IS *changing.*

The girls can go out on a Friday night and, for 30 Euro, look like a billion dollars for 24 hours. That's the facts of life! Wear something twice and then throw it away.

These big companies like H&M, while they are a necessary part of evolution, they are ruining my fate. I have no problem saying it. They are really doing it. I did it before, at a big company, so I know the ins and outs of these people. H&M, they're destroying something.

H+M

THERE ARE 62 H+Ms IN AUSTRIA, A COUNTRY WITH THE SAME POPULATION AS CHICAGO, *which has three.* (4)

The [companies] will say, they are protecting working places in India or in China, but that is not quite a true thing. You're destroying a lot more. I have seen it. I was in India, for ten years, every 6-8 weeks.

In addition to H&Ms, there are 19 Mango-affiliated outlets, two Forever21 locales, and five Zara stores in Vienna proper, with four elsewhere in the country. (5)

The only way to describe what H&M is doing is abusing the human relationship. [The workers] really have a terrible life. You know, if men would be working in the textile industry, on the sewing machines, you'd go broke tomorrow. **The girls have stamina.**

These girls come home, 6 pm, from work. The husband is half sozzled—especially in Mauritius. Then she has to make dinner, look after the kids ... she falls into bed, and 5 o'clock she gets up again. It's a terrible life for a woman. And when you pay them peanuts ... I worked it out once, it's about 30 cents an hour. I find it very, very ... I find it disgusting, actually.

E. BRAUN & Co.

INDIAN GARMENT WORKERS EARN ABOUT 64 EURO PER MONTH, OR 43% OF A LIVING WAGE. (6)

The people who are buying these goods, in Austria and Germany, they're not informed. We cannot sustain [that]. We have a moral obligation to society.

SALE!

Working with men is sometimes very frustrating. Men don't know their colors. Women customers come and buy for their men—they know their colors. Not everything is handmade anymore, and anyway who wants suits for 5,000 Euro? Even if you have the money, that's getting to the point where it's ridiculous. [Men also] have a messed up system in the brain department, where he thinks, "if he's nicely dressed, he must be a homosexual." It's so wrong.

Although wages of domestic workers, au pairs, and janitorial staff fall below this line, most workers in Austria earn no less than 1,000 Euro per month. (7)

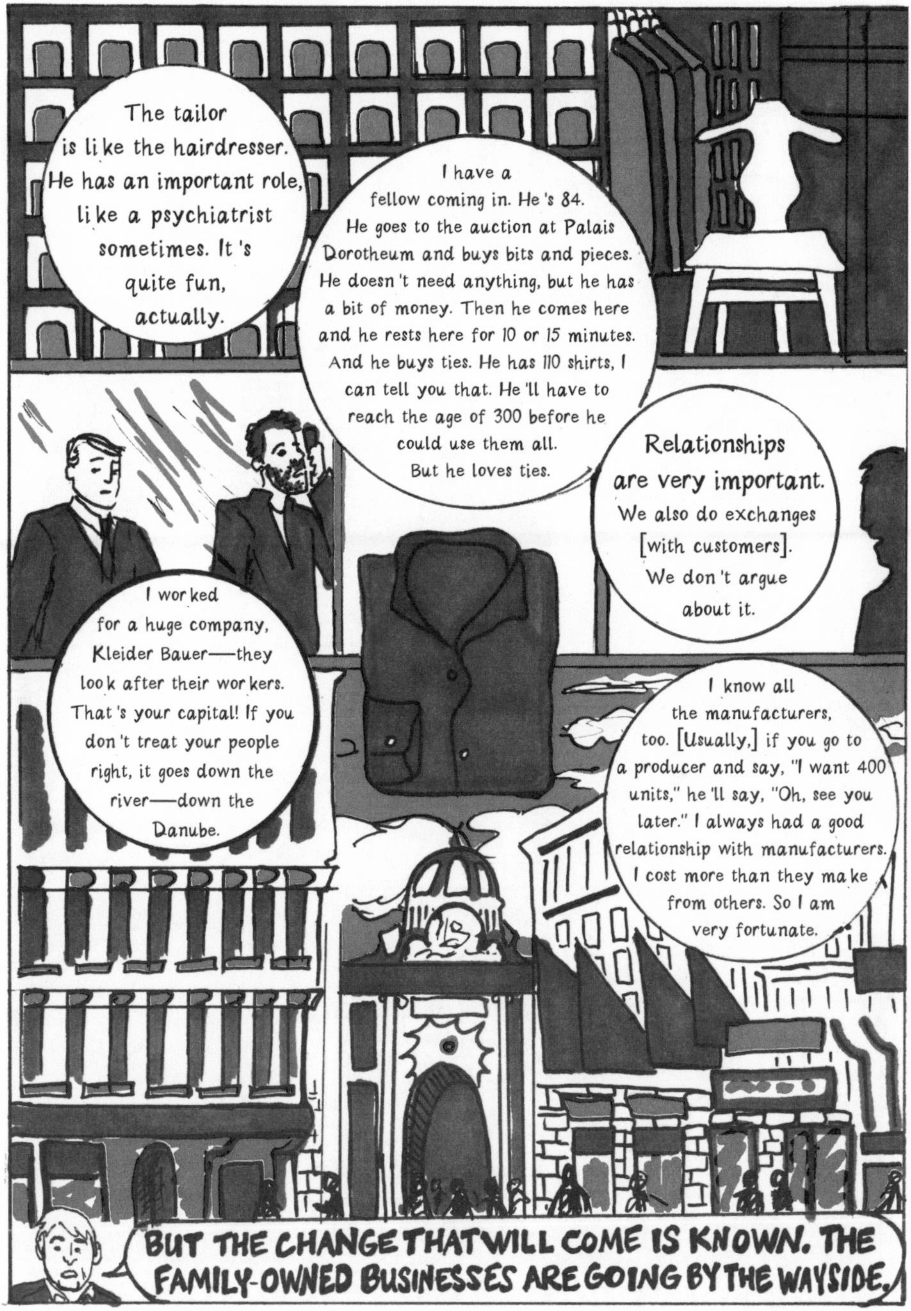
The tailor is like the hairdresser. He has an important role, like a psychiatrist sometimes. It's quite fun, actually.
I have a fellow coming in. He's 84. He goes to the auction at Palais Dorotheum and buys bits and pieces. He doesn't need anything, but he has a bit of money. Then he comes here and he rests here for 10 or 15 minutes. And he buys ties. He has 110 shirts, I can tell you that. He'll have to reach the age of 300 before he could use them all. But he loves ties.
Relationships are very important. We also do exchanges [with customers]. We don't argue about it.
I worked for a huge company, Kleider Bauer—they look after their workers. That's your capital! If you don't treat your people right, it goes down the river—down the Danube.
I know all the manufacturers, too. [Usually,] if you go to a producer and say, "I want 400 units," he'll say, "Oh, see you later." I always had a good relationship with manufacturers. I cost more than they make from others. So I am very fortunate.
BUT THE CHANGE THAT WILL COME IS KNOWN. THE FAMILY-OWNED BUSINESSES ARE GOING BY THE WAYSIDE.

WRITTEN BY: ANNE ELIZABETH MOORE ◆ DRAWN BY: DELIA JEAN

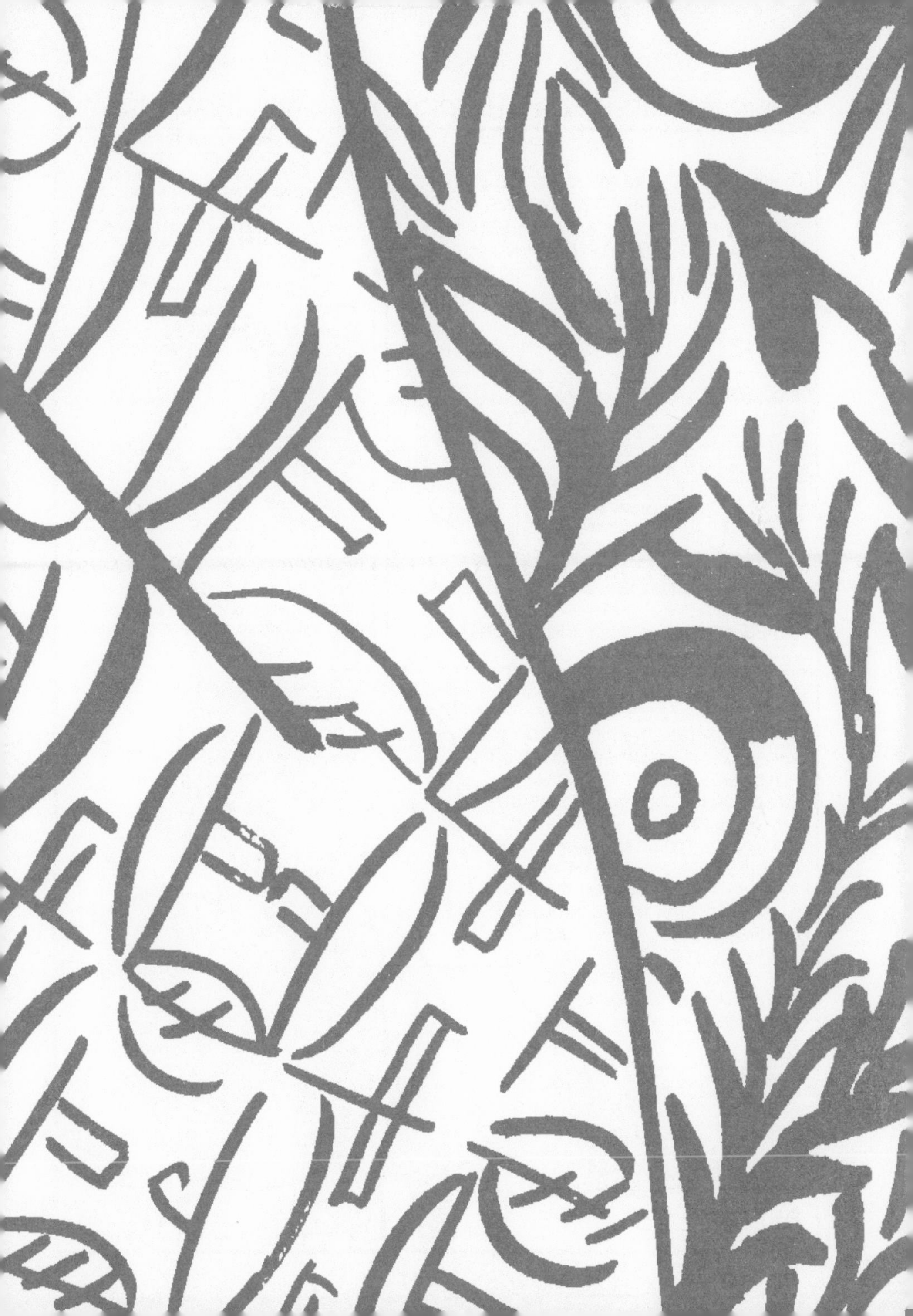

ANGELA VOELKER, TEXTILE HISTORIAN / CURATOR (FORMER MAK)

(WHEN I WAS AT) THE MUSEUM,* WE INHERITED THE WIENER WERKSTAETTE ARCHIVES, AND THEY HAD A WONDERFUL TEXTILE PRODUCTION, AND ALSO FASHION. I WORK ON LACE AND EMBROIDERY. IT'S A SPECIALTY FIELD. THEY DID A LOT OF CUSHIONS. (1)

* THE MAK, OR MUSEUM OF APPLIED ARTS.

IN THE WIENER WERKSTAETTE, A LOT OF THE ARTISTS WERE WOMEN, A LOT OF THE ONES WHO DID THE ACTUAL NEEDLEWORK WERE WOMEN. BUT A LOT OF THESE MODERN MACHINES WERE WORKED BY MEN. PUTTING THINGS ON THE LOOM AND WORKING WITH IT THIS WAS MENS' WORK.

ALTHOUGH THE GARMENT INDUSTRY WORLDWIDE ONLY HAS ABOUT A **10%** MALE WORKFORCE, ABOUT **40%** OF THE 20,000 EMPLOYEES IN TEXTILES, APPAREL, AND FOOTWEAR IN AUSTRIA ARE MALE. (2)

THERE ARE PLACES. BACKHAUSEN, WHICH IS NOT OWNED BY BACKHAUSEN ANYMORE, AND WALDVIERTLER. THERE IS A FIRM THAT PRINTS TEXTILES FOR NIGERIA. IT STARTED IN THE 1960S. SOME TRADE COMMISSIONER FOR NIGERIA ASKED COMPANIES TO PROVIDE PRODUCTS FOR NIGERIA. THEY NEVER ENTERED AUSTRIAN MARKETS. MOST PEOPLE DON'T EVEN KNOW IT HAPPENED - IT WAS STRICTLY FOR EXPORT. ALSO, I DON'T THINK ANYONE WOULD HAVE BEEN BUYING THESE THINGS BECAUSE THEY WERE OUTRAGEOUSLY COLORFUL. IT'S CALLED LACE, ALTHOUGH IT'S MACHINE EMBROIDERY. IT'S QUITE WILD. (3)

BUT OF COURSE MOST OF THE INDUSTRY IS GONE.

DECORATION HAS ALWAYS BEEN IMPORTANT IN AUSTRIAN TEXTILES.

PEOPLE IN AUSTRIA WERE ALWAYS INTERESTED IN HAVING HANDCRAFTED OBJECTS. THIS THING OF BEING OFFENDED BY INDUSTRIAL PRODUCTION DATES ALREADY FROM THE 19TH CENTURY. THE MACHINES CAME INTO AUSTRIA RATHER LATE.

PEOPLE TRIED TO WEAVE VERY CHEAPLY, IN PRIVATE HOMES, AND THEY DIDN'T FEEL THE NEED TO HAVE A LARGER PRODUCTION. BY THE MIDDLE OF THE CENTURY THERE WERE POWER LOOMS, BUT COMPARED TO OTHER COUNTRIES, IT TOOK A LONG TIME BEFORE THIS WAS COMMON. IT CAME OUT OF FEAR OF LOSING THEIR DOMAINS, THEIR WORK. THE WIENER WERKSTAETTE AND OTHER FIRMS COULD RELY ON VERY WELL-TRAINED ARTISANS OR HANDICRAFT PEOPLE. THEY STILL LEARNED OLD TECHNIQUES BESIDE THE INDUSTRIAL REVOLUTION.

NOWADAYS, I THINK IT'S HARD TO FIND A DIFFERENCE BETWEEN AUSTRIA AND ANY OTHER COUNTRY. I'VE BEEN HERE FOR 40 YEARS, AND WHEN I CAME HERE IT WAS COMMON TO FIND TAILORS FOR AVERAGE PEOPLE, WHICH I THINK IS NOW VERY RARE.

THERE ARE PEOPLE INTERESTED IN FASHION. BUT THEY, OF COURSE, HAD INTERNATIONAL TEACHERS. NO VIENNESE, EXCEPT HELMUT LANG, WHO I THINK WAS ABSENT THE ENTIRE SEMESTER.

FITTING

OPEN

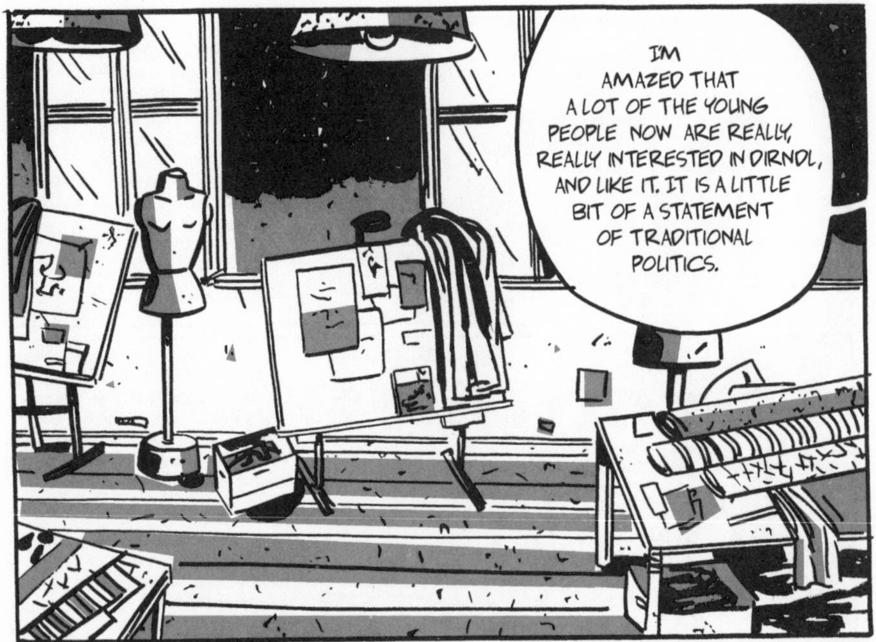
I'M AMAZED THAT A LOT OF THE YOUNG PEOPLE NOW ARE REALLY, REALLY INTERESTED IN DIRNDL, AND LIKE IT. IT IS A LITTLE BIT OF A STATEMENT OF TRADITIONAL POLITICS.

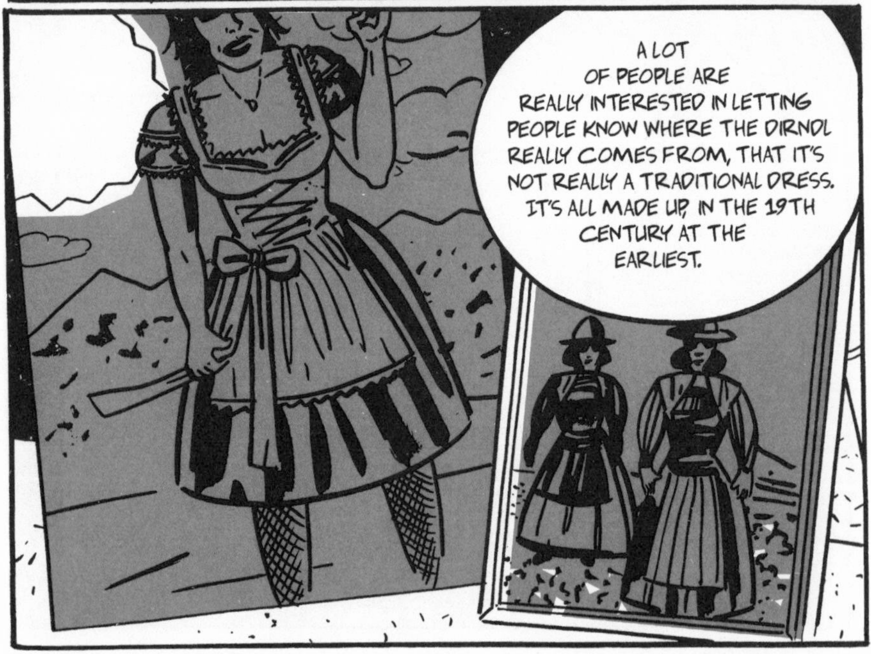
A LOT OF PEOPLE ARE REALLY INTERESTED IN LETTING PEOPLE KNOW WHERE THE DIRNDL REALLY COMES FROM, THAT IT'S NOT REALLY A TRADITIONAL DRESS. IT'S ALL MADE UP, IN THE 19TH CENTURY AT THE EARLIEST.

THERE WAS AN INTERESTING EXHIBITION UP AT THE VOLKSKUNDEMUSEUM OF EMBROIDERIES OF UKRAINIAN REFUGEES. THE REFUGEES WERE TAKEN FROM THE UKRAINE AND PUT INTO CAMPS, AND TRAINED TO DO EMBROIDERIES. THEY WERE TAUGHT, OR THE PEOPLE THAT TAUGHT THEM —UKRAINIANS AND ALSO AUSTRIANS— WERE TAUGHT, THAT THESE WERE TRADITIONAL EMBROIDERIES. IT WAS NOT AT ALL THEIR TRADITION, BUT MADE UP BY PEOPLE WHO THOUGHT IT COULD BE A PART OF THEIR HERITAGE. IT GOES TOGETHER WITH THE FALL OF THE EMPIRE, WHERE ALL OF THESE SMALLER COUNTRIES HAD NATIONALISTIC IDEAS, AND WANTED TO GET RID OF THE HAPSBURGS. THAT WAS WHY THE MONARCHY COLLAPSED. BUT THE IDEA WAS TO DO SOME GOOD, TO HELP THESE PEOPLE TAKE PART IN SMALL INDUSTRIES AND EARN MORE MONEY.

THE HISTORY OF THE DIRNDL IS SIMILAR. WHAT'S COMING OUT NOW IS THAT THE HISTORY OF THE DIRNDL AS AUSTRIAN WAS ALL CONSTRUCTED. YOUNGER PEOPLE HAVE THEIR DIFFERENT MOMENTS. THEIR DIRNDL MOMENTS, THEIR JEANS MOMENTS. THEY DON'T HAVE ANY OF THESE IDEAS ABOUT FASCISM AND NAZIS. IN GERMANY, PEOPLE ARE MUCH MORE ANXIOUS THAT THEY SHOULDN'T WEAR THIS KIND OF FASHION.

WRITTEN BY ANNE ELIZABETH MOORE / DRAWN BY SIMON HÄUSSLE

CONNIE, URBAN PLANNER

My dad ran a textile plant, a carpet manufacturer. They started out making carpet for private houses, but people don't have carpets in their houses anymore. They have wood. Most of the things they do [now are] for industry. (1)

My great grandfather also ran a factory. In his factory, they recycled cotton—from old garments, they made new garments. For the military, because it was the beginning of the last century. The whole family is in the textile industry.

 THE ONLY THING THAT COMES FROM THAT IS THAT I LIKE COTTON. I LIKE TO WEAR IT.

I THINK AUSTRIA IS LEADING IN TRADITIONAL CLOTHING—LIKE DIRNDL.

Over 80% of what's called "country-style fashion" produced in Austria—including dirndl, Loden, boiled wool jackets, linen dresses—is exported, primarily to Germany. (2)

About five years ago, young people started wearing dirndl and traditional costumes. It's a conservative backlash, I think. Very traditional gender roles. I really like wearing [mine] but I don't have a very traditional one. It's more of a fashion dirndl.

Designer Lena Hoschek, a former assistant to Hollywood costume designer Vivienne Westwood, launched her own dirndl-heavy clothing line in Graz in 2004, then opened a storefront in Vienna in 2007.

THE DIRNDL IS A VERY SEXY OUTFIT, BUT MOST OF THE YOUNG PEOPLE NOW, THEY REALLY WEAR IT SERIOUSLY.

(Westwood once famously said, "There would be no ugliness in the world if every woman wore a dirndl.")

A lot of people that are wearing dirndl are coming from the former Yugoslavia, say. It is not only Austrians by birth that are wearing this. So it is more [complicated] than nationalism. The dirndl is kind of a symbol. It's really like the 1950s. It says, I am a good wife, I am tidy and neat.

I'M OFTEN ASKED WHY I DIDN'T MOVE TO LONDON, PARIS, OR MILAN, "HOSCHECK ONCE SAID. "BUT THERE'S NOWHERE IN THE WORLD I COULD WORK AS CREATIVELY AS AUSTRIA." (3)

It's about being conservative, and Austrian, and narrow-minded. I think it goes hand-in-hand with political developments. [The men's costume has a similar message]: Strong. Rural. Tough. Jörg Haider in Corinthia was always wearing things like that.

But traditional dress, while unique, makes up only a small part of the contemporary Austrian textile industry.

[In general, Austrian men] dress better than the Germans. Oh, that is a very Austrian thing to say. I think they decide what they wear by what is comfortable.

Companies housed in Austria also produce—or import—sportswear, bedding and homewear, business attire, casual apparel, and lingerie.

YOU ONLY HAVE TO GO TO THE GRABEN, IN THE FIRST DISTRICT, WHERE YOU HAVE AN H+M IN THE OLD FASHION HOUSE E. BRAUN+C° THAT SAYS A LOT.

E. BRAUN + C°.

H+M

Of Austrian brands named on the World Fashion Website, a listing for noteworthy apparel and adornment offerings from countries around the world, there are nearly four times as many business attire companies as country-style fashion retailers.

My mother told me the story of Conchita Wurst. I did not know it. About six years ago, Tom Neuwirth entered a talent show like The Voice——I think he got second place, but he didn't win. Then there was another talent show, and another. Then he thought, I need to change something. So, another talent show [Die grosse Chance], and he entered as Conchita Wurst. But he didn't win.

Then, I don't know how it worked out, but the ÖRF decided that he will attend the Eurovision Songwriting Contest as Conchita Wurst. Normally, the contest is decided by voting.

Tom Neuwirth got a whole group of I think German composers and they wrote a song especially for the song contest. It took about one and a half years. It was really branded for the song contest.

Now that we have Conchita Wurst, everything can change!

(A surprising number of lingerie producers in Austria still offer traditional corsetry.)

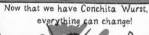

Actually, I think it's interesting. He, or she, is from Bad Mitterndorf, the hotspot of traditional life in Austria. The hot hot hot hotspot. The whole community of Bad Mitterndorf really supports Conchita Wurst.

When she won, [a news program asked], What would you think if your son was like Conchita Wurst? And everyone said they would like it. I don't think they would really like it, but it's such a hype now that [they say] it's OK.

I think a lot of people don't know he's a guy. They think he's a girl. But my gay friends, they all say, It's really great for us. He really is a drag artist. Trans [issues] are not his message. I think, never, ever would Austria send a transgender person to the song contest. But people really mix things up.

As a [fashion icon, she] is very elegant. The figure [Thomas Neuwirth] created is really interesting because normally a drag artist is very loud, extraverted, and weird. Conchita Wurst is very silent. All the things she's saying——there's no provocation. It's more asexual. That's interesting, I think, because it's completely neutral.

WRITTEN BY ANNE ELIZABETH MOORE / DRAWN BY DELIA JEAN

I'M FROM VORARLBERG. MOSTLY I GREW UP AWARE OF APPAREL AS AN INDUSTRY THAT WAS OVER. I THINK THE HISTORY OF THE TEXTILE INDUSTRY THERE MADE PEOPLE REALLY CONSCIOUS OF WHAT THEY BUY. THEY LIKE GOOD CLOTHES, GOOD QUALITY. THEY SHOP CONSCIOUSLY. (1)

THE WESTERN-MOST REGION OF AUSTRIA WAS TRADITIONALLY THE COUNTRY'S GARMENT-PRODUCING CAPITAL. IT IS ALSO THE WEALTHIEST IN THE NATION.

BUT LIKE EVERYWHERE, THE LOWER CLASSES ARE GROWING. THERE'S NOT SO MUCH MONEY, EVEN THERE, AS THERE USED TO BE. SO THEY THINK, "OH, WE CAN ONLY SHOP AT H+M." EVEN THOUGH THEY HAVE MORE MONEY THAN THE REST OF AUSTRIA.

AGRICULTURE, ELECTRONICS, MACHINERY AND PACKING MATERIALS HAVE PICKED UP SOME OF THE SLACK, BUT EVEN WITH THE DECLINE OF THE INDUSTRY, THE REGION STILL MANUFACTURES MOST TEXTILES MADE IN THE COUNTRY.

BEFORE I WAS DOING COMICS, I WAS WORKING AS A PAINTER, LIKE A HOUSE PAINTER. I WAS AN EMPLOYEE OF A COMPANY. IT WAS ALL ABOUT HIGH QUALITY WORK FOR UPPER CLASS CUSTOMERS.

AND OF COURSE, YOU'RE AROUND MEN IN THIS CIRCLE THAT HAVE THIS REALLY... I WOULDN'T SAY MACHO, BUT THEY'RE JUST MEN. THERE'S NO GAYNESS, THERE'S NO IDEA OF EQUALITY. IT'S JUST "US MEN" AT WORK. AND YOU SAW IT IN THE WAY THEY DRESSED.

THERE WAS NEVER A QUESTION OF STYLE, IT WAS JUST, HOW TO LOOK COOL. BLACK PANTS, BLACK SHIRTS. DURING THE DAY YOU WERE JUST IN YOUR WORK WEAR. WHITE PANTS, WHITE T-SHIRT. THE MORE CLEAN YOU WERE, THE MORE PROF-ESSIONAL YOU WERE.

THEY WERE A REALLY CLOSE CIRCLE OF PEOPLE, BUT THEY ALSO HAD A TIGHT-KNIT ATTITUDE THAT YOU COULDN'T GET OUT OF. IF SOMEBODY WANTED TO DO SOMETHING DIFFERENT - I'M NOT EVEN TALKING ABOUT MYSELF. IF SOMEBODY ELSE CAME IN DOING AN INTERNSHIP AND THEY WERE INTO ALTERNATIVE STUFF, THE WHOLE CREW RIPPED ON THEM.

"OH, YOU GOT COLORFUL HAIR," OR "WHY DO YOU LISTEN TO THE STUFF YOU LISTEN TO."

WRITTEN BY ANNE ELIZABETH MOORE / DRAWN BY SIMON HAÜSSLE

THAT REALLY PUT A STAMP ON ME FOR THAT TIME. I KNOW I'M NOT DRESSED IN THE RADDEST ATTIRE MYSELF BUT AT LEAST I HAVE AN APPRECIATION FOR ALL KINDS OF PEOPLE. I THINK I DRESS REGULAR. JEANS, CHUCKS, AND A T-SHIRT. BUT UNDERGROUND PEOPLE, OR PEOPLE INTO ALTERNATIVE CULTURE, THAT ALL SHOP IN THRIFT STORES OR BUY NON-LABEL CLOTHES, THEY STILL END UP WEARING BLACK PANTS OR JEANS, WITH A SHIRT OR A T-SHIRT. EVERYONE THINKS THEY'RE SO INDIVIDUAL BUT I THINK IT'S ALSO A UNIFORM. NOW THAT I'M WORKING IN BOOKS, I DON'T GET OUT SO MUCH, BUT I USED TO BE REALLY SENSITIVE ABOUT THIS EARLIER ON.

"WHY DO YOU DRESS SO CRAPPY? YOU'RE LIVING IN A RICH COUNTRY, YOU HAVE A CHOICE. YOU CAN AFFORD STUFF" I THINK PEOPLE ARE HAPPY THEY DON'T HAVE TO CHOOSE.

(FAST FASHION) CAME SLOWLY TO VORARLBERG. IT TOOK ABOUT 15 YEARS FOR IT TO REALLY SPREAD FROM VIENNA. WE DIDN'T REALLY SHOP THERE. WE WENT TO THE PERSON WHO BOUGHT THE FABRIC FOR THEIR STORE, YOU KNOW, WE KNOW HIM, WE SUPPORT HIM, THIS IS HOW WE DO IT, HERE. H+M YOU WOULD ONLY GO TO IF YOU WERE STARTING A NEW LIFE AS A STUDENT AND YOU NEED CHEAP CLOTHES. THERE WAS THIS ATTITUDE WHEN YOU WOULD SEE REALLY CHEAP CLOTHING STORES, THAT ONLY THE POOR PEOPLE GO THERE. SO THERE WAS ALWAYS A LOOKING-DOWN ATTITUDE FOR THE PEOPLE WHO GO THERE.

VORARLBERG FACTORY, DORNBIRN 1910

AT THE SAME TIME, THE TEXTILE INDUSTRY... IT SORT OF WITHDREW. THE EVIL MULTINATIONALS TOOK IT AWAY, TOO, BUT IT JUST SORT OF WITHDREW. THEY DIDN'T REALLY PREPARE THEMSELVES FOR THE CHANGE. THEY JUST SOMEHOW LET GO.

TODAY, AROUND 70% OF THE APPAREL MADE IN AUSTRIA IS EXPORTED, MOSTLY TO GERMANY AND OTHER PLACES IN EUROPE.

Endnotes for Chapter Two

Die Arbeitslosen Von Marienthal

1. From the Foreword to the American Edition by Paul F. Lazarsfeld. Marie Jahoda, Paul F. Lazarsfeld, and Hans Zeisel. *Marienthal: The Sociography of an Unemployed Community*, Aldine Atherton, Inc. (Chicago, 1971). P. vii.

2. Ibid, pp. 11-14.

3. Ibid, p. 14.

4. Ibid, p. vii.

5. Ibid, p. 38.

6. Ibid, p. x.

7. Ibid, p. 74.

8. Ibid, p. 74.

9. Ibid, p. 67.

10. Ibid, p. 67.

11. Ibid, p. 67.

12. Ibid, p. 22.

13. Ibid, p. 26.

14. Ibid, p. 77.

15. Ibid, p. 76.

16. Ibid, p. 76.

17. Ibid, p. 76.

Andrea Komlosy, Researcher

1. All quotes, unless otherwise attributed, are from an interview between Andrea Komlosy and Anne Elizabeth Moore conducted May 30, 2014, in Vienna, Austria.

2. "Facts and Figures: Textile Industry," Advantage Austria. http://www.advan-

tageaustria.org/international/zentral/business-guide-oesterreich/importieren-aus-oes-terreich/branchen/mode-und-textilien/zahlen-und-fakten.en.html (accessed September 15, 2015).

Johann Perzi, Tailor

1. "About," Philippe Perzi, Vienna. http://philippeperzi.com/about/the-story/ (accessed September 15, 2015).

2. All quotes, unless otherwise attributed, are from an interview between Johann Perzi and Anne Elizabeth Moore conducted on June 10, 2014 in Vienna, Austria.

3. Home page, Philippe Perzi, Vienna. http://philippeperzi.com (accessed September 15, 2015).

4. Personal count from H&M corporate website, Austria, May 19, 2014. http://www.hm.com/at/store-locator#

5. Personal count from corporate websites, conducted May 19, 2014.

6. "Indian garment workers exploited, says tribunal." *Pravasi Mathrubhumi*, November 26, 2012. http://www.mathrubhumi.com/english/news/business/indian-garment-workers-exploited-says-tribunal-130539.html (accessed September 15, 2015).

7. An Austrian minimum wage of 1,000 Euros went into effect in 2009, although off-books employment means some workers fall short of this minimum. See "Average Salary in European Union," Reinis Fischer, July 20, 2015. http://www.reinisfischer.com/average-salary-european-union-2015 (accessed September 15, 2015).

Angela Voelker

1. All quotes, unless otherwise attributed, are from an interview between Angela Voelker and Anne Elizabeth Moore conducted June 4 2014, in Vienna, Austria.

2. "Facts and Figures: Textile Industry," *Advantage Austria*. http://www.advantageaustria.org/international/zentral/business-guide-oesterreich/importieren-aus-oes-terreich/branchen/mode-und-textilien/zahlen-und-fakten.en.html (accessed Septem-

ber 15, 2015).

3. For more on this, see Plankensteiner, Barbara, "African Lace: An industrial fabric connecting Austria and Nigeria," *Anthrovision*, January 2, 2013. http://anthrovision. revues.org/679 (accessed September 15, 2015).

Connie, Urban Planner

1. All quotes, unless otherwise attributed, are from an interview between Connie Brendt and Anne Elizabeth Moore conducted May 27, 2014, in Vienna, Austria.

2. "Overview: Fashion and Textiles," *Advantage Austria*. http://www.advantageaustria.org (accessed October 1, 2014).

3. "Dirndl goes high fashion," *Austria Arrive and Revive*. http://www.austria.info/au/people-and-traditions/lena-hoschek-1881256.html (accessed October 1, 2014).

Simon, Cartoonist

1. All quotes are from an interview between Simon Häussle and Anne Elizabeth Moore conducted May 27 2014, in Vienna, Austria.

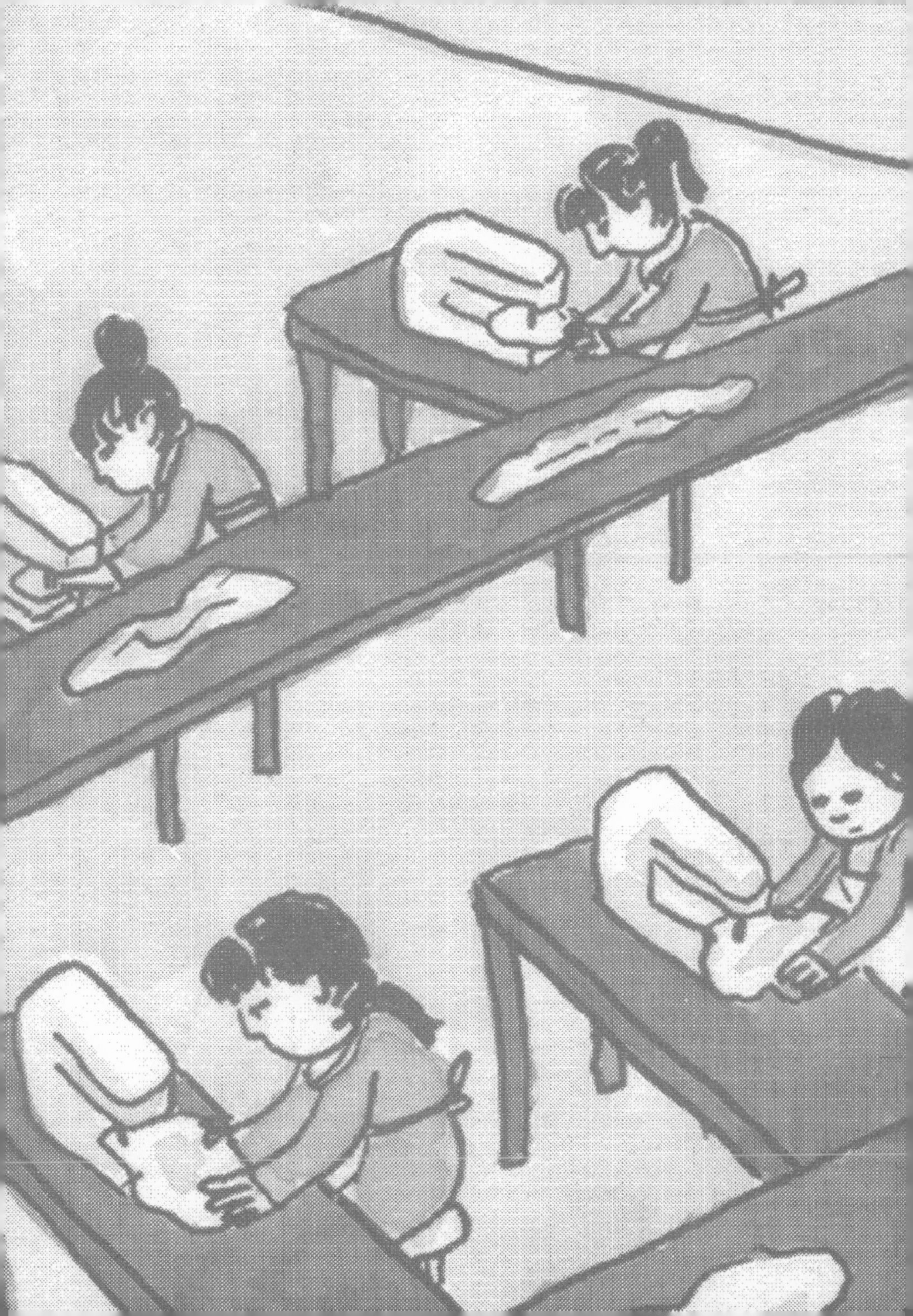

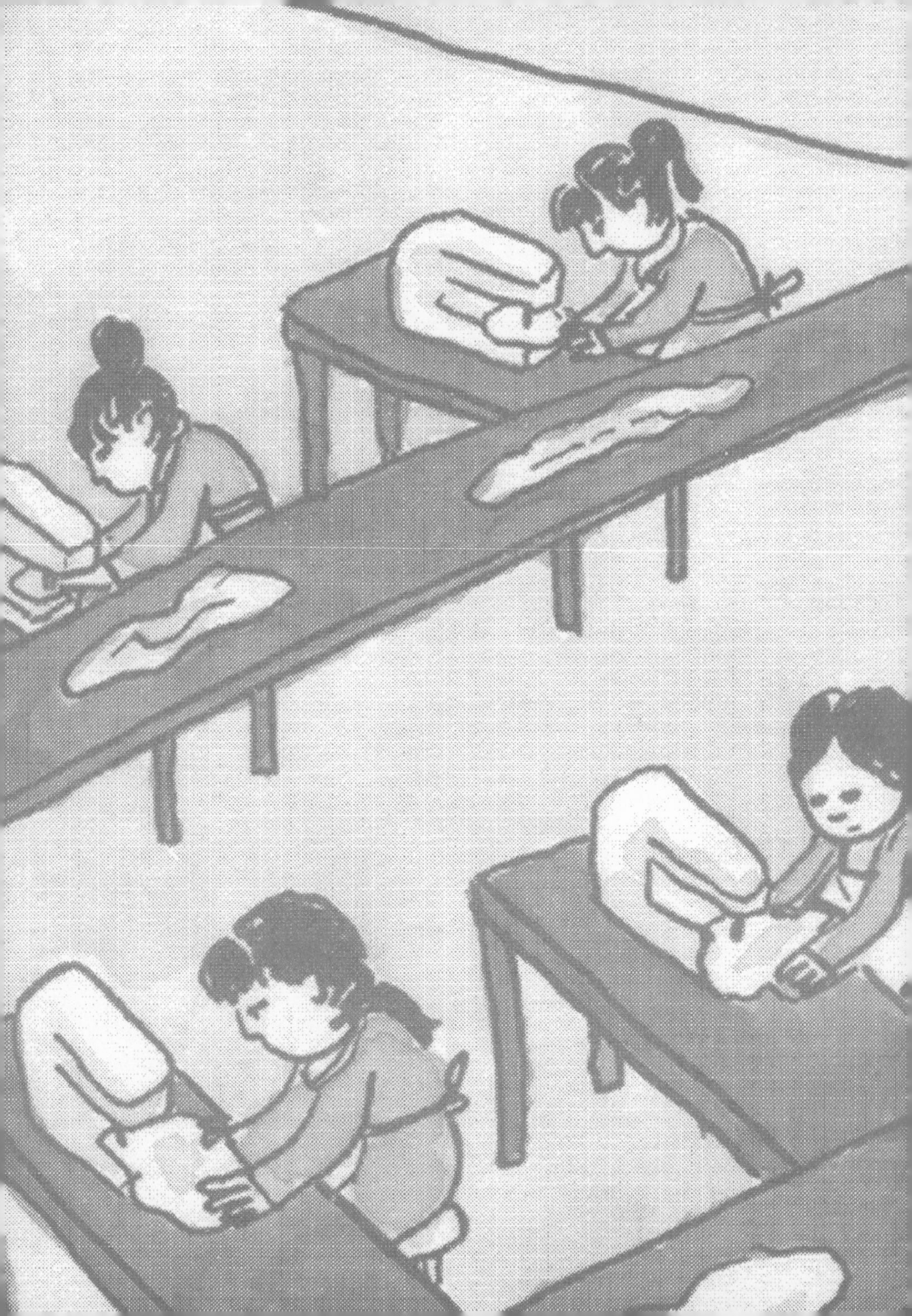

Chapter 3 : Cambodia

I knew when I started the comics journalism series for *Truthout* that I would be returning to Phnom Penh during the run of strips; I did not know that my plane would land on the first day of the largest garment worker strike in Cambodia's history. Even further from my mind was any awareness that these uprisings would end so violently. Had I been gifted with foresight (and a touch more cynicism), it might have further crossed my mind that the events I would experience after I stepped off the plane at Pochentong International would go on to provide the perfect object lesson to the story I was tracking. From a remove, it was completely clear: the international policies that drive production of U.S. and EU-consumed apparel offshore and keep wages too low and options too limited for far too many women in the world are driving national and industrial leaders to kill those same women when they speak up about low wages and bad working conditions. There is no alternative reading.

On January 3, 2014, military police opened fire at a Special Economic Zone on the outskirts of Phnom Penh and killed at least five garment workers, injured over 40, and arrested 10. Others remain missing to this day, and corroborating, if unofficially recognized, reports about a sixth body have emerged. (See Melissa Mendes' "Outta Sight! (Outta Mind)," on page 85.) The country was devastated; over half the nation, keep in mind, had survived the Khmer Rouge regime and had personal, visceral experience with state violence. I was also devastated; I had been meeting with and interviewing protestors for weeks on this trip; years, if we count previous excursions to the city. These were people I cared about deeply, and their government had just shot them. I forgot, almost entirely, about this project.

An immediate ban on gatherings of more than 10 people in any location was enacted, in an effort to quell the organizing that can emerge from crass displays of aggression such as the citizenship of Phnom Penh had just experienced. I was teaching at a college; I had 12 students. Class was effectively cancelled by government decree. I had nothing to do.

Had the apparel strike continued without violent intervention, in other words, I would have been occupied with other duties on January 4, 2014. I would never have found occasion to visit an anti-sex trafficking NGO that sits just a few kilometers south of Canadia Industrial Park, where the protestors had just been shot. I would never have entered the facility that claims to offer human trafficking victims a life free of enslavement; never would have realized that what a "life free of enslavement" means to this and many other NGOs around the world was a job in the garment factories. Just the day before it had become clear that a life in the garment factories was not one free of violence, danger, or coercion. Ironically, had the garment workers' uprising been allowed to continue, I would never have stumbled across the deep influence the apparel industry holds over organizations that seek to respond to human trafficking. (I won't tell you any more about it here; you'll get much more out of Ellen Lindner's amazing depictions starting on page 91.)

For NGOs to associate with the garment industry is not a crime: appallingly low wages paid to supposed victims of sex trafficking—lower even than factory work—should be but isn't, either. More distressing, at the NGO I visited the day after the strikes ended, I witnessed consistent confusion about what exactly constituted sex trafficking, as well as the regular misgendering of clients. These conflicting statements, aptly illustrated by Leela Corman in "The Grey Area," (page 102) reflect larger problems. Not only do they signal concerns regarding funding that international donors may wish to keep in mind, but they could constitute human rights violations. And those are crimes.

OUTTA SIGHT! (Outta mind.)

WRITTEN BY
ANNE ELIZABETH MOORE

DRAWN BY
MELISSA MENDES

OFFSHORE MANUFACTURERS WHO CLOTHE THE WORLD DIDN'T GET INTO THE APPAREL GAME BECAUSE THEY HAD IMMEDIATE ACCESS TO NECESSARY RESOURCES, LIKE COTTON OR SPANDEX

or models.

MANY WERE LURED BY US OR EU TRADE AGREEMENTS. THE TERMS OF THE 1974 MULTI-FIBRE AGREEMENT (MFA), FOR EXAMPLE, CONVINCED BANGLADESH TO START BUILDING FACTORIES. A FEW DECADES LATER, STILL EMERGING FROM CIVIL WAR, CAMBODIA FOLLOWED SUIT. HAITI, WHICH HAS EXPORTED APPAREL SINCE THE 1980'S, RECENTLY ENTERED INTO A PREFERENTIAL FREE-TRADE DEAL OFFERING DUTY-FREE APPAREL IMPORTS TO THE US— THE HAITIAN ECONOMIC LIFT PROGRAM ACT (HELP) –THROUGH 2020.

BANGLADESH

HAITI

NATURAL RESOURCES: GOLD, COPPER

NATURAL RESOURCES: MANGOES, NATURAL GAS

CAMBODIA

NATURAL RESOURCES: TIMBER, RICE

THE QUOTAS OFFERED UNDER THE MFA GAVE DEVELOPING NATIONS A FAIR SHOT AT EXPORTING APPAREL TO THE MOST LUCRATIVE MARKETS. HELP OFFERS DIFFERENT BENEFITS WITH THE SAME RESULT: MORE GARMENT PRODUCTION FOR US AND EU CONSUMPTION.

WHEN APPAREL MANUFACTURING GLOBALIZED, CHEAP LABOR BECAME MORE IMPORTANT TO THE GARMENT TRADE, AND NATIONAL GOVERNMENTS DEVELOPED A KEEN INTEREST IN MAKING SURE THEY COULD PROVIDE IT.

MOST OTHER NECESSARY MATERIALS ARE SHIPPED IN. THERE AREN'T MANY NATURAL RESOURCES AVAILABLE WHERE PRODUCTION NOW OCCURS. IN FACT, THE ONLY RELEVANT "NATURAL" RESOURCE MANY OF THE WORLD'S BIGGEST GARMENT EXPORTERS HAVE ACCESS TO IS PEOPLE IN POVERTY.

MANUFACTURING ASSOCIATIONS ARE THEREFORE POWERFUL LOBBIES, WITH A GREAT DEAL OF INFLUENCE OVER GOVERNMENTAL REACTION TO LABOR CONCERNS. THE BANGLADESH GARMENT MANUFACTURERS AND EXPORTERS ASSOCIATION, FOR EXAMPLE, LISTS NEARLY 3000 FACTORY-OWNING MEMBERS ON THEIR WEBSITE. (MORE THAN 20 OF THEM ARE MEMBERS OF PARLIAMENT.) (1) THEY REPRESENT 5,600 FACTORIES AND EMPLOY 4 MILLION WORKERS, WHO MAKE 80% OF THE COUNTRY'S EXPORTS.

THAT'S 200 MORE SINCE THE TAZREEN FACTORY FIRE IN NOVEMBER 2012 AND THE RANA PLAZA COLLAPSE SEVEN MONTHS LATER KILLED A COMBINED TOTAL OF OVER 1200 WORKERS IN BANGLADESH FACTORIES. GARMENT EXPORTS, TOO INCREASED 24% DURING THAT TIME. (2) UNSURPRISINGLY, TRANSPARENCY INTERNATIONAL (TI) RATED BANGLADESH THE 136th MOST CORRUPT OF 177 NATIONS IN 2013.

TI PLACED CAMBODIA ON THE SAME LIST. AT A TENTH THE POPULATION OF BANGLADESH, ITS APPAREL WORKFORCE IS A TENTH THE SIZE, TOO — 400,000 WORKERS. ALTHOUGH THE GARMENT MANUFACTURING ASSOCIATION OF CAMBODIA IS POWERFUL—THE INDUSTRY ACCOUNTS FOR 80% OF THE NATION'S EXPORTS—MANY FACTORY OWNERS ARE FOREIGN, WHICH MEANS A BULK OF THEIR PROFITS DON'T EVEN STAY IN COUNTRY. SUBCONTRACTING, ALSO COMMON IN CAMBODIA, MEANS MONITORED FACTORIES MAY OUTSOURCE WORK TO UNMONITORED, OR "BLACK" FACTORIES. THESE MAY NOT HAVE PROPER EXPORTING LICENSES, BUT SOME WORKERS NEVER KNOW THE DIFFERENCE.

HAITI FARED WORST WITH TI— IT'S LISTED AS THE 163rd MOST CORRUPT OF 177 COUNTRIES. ITS POPULATION AND INDUSTRY ARE MUCH SMALLER, BUT A FULL 42% OF THE COUNTRY'S EXPORTS ARE T-SHIRTS. (3) THESE, IN COMBINATION WITH OTHER APPAREL ITEMS, MAKE UP 90% OF HAITI'S EXPORTS. (4)

OWNERS AND MANAGERS REMAIN OVERWHELMINGLY MALE—THERE ARE ONLY A HANDFUL OF FEMALE FACTORY OWNERS IN CAMBODIA, FOR EXAMPLE, AND NONE ARE CAMBODIAN—BUT APPROXIMATELY 90% OF THE CAMBODIAN WORKFORCE IS FEMALE, 80% OF THE BANGLADESHI, AND 64% OF THE HAITIAN.

钱是个好！

UNIONS TEND TO NEGLECT WOMEN'S PARTICIPATION. ALTHOUGH BANGLADESH HAS NEARLY 7,000 GARMENT WORKER UNIONS IN 32 FEDERATIONS, WOMEN MADE UP ONLY 14% OF MEMBERS IN 2009. (5) THAT SAME YEAR, CAMBODIA HAD APPROXIMATELY 1,000 UNIONS IN 27 FEDERATIONS, AND 55% WOMEN'S PARTICIPATION—ALTHOUGH WOMEN HELD FEW POSITIONS OF LEADERSHIP. (6)

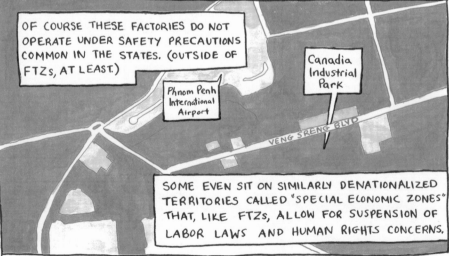

OF COURSE THESE FACTORIES DO NOT OPERATE UNDER SAFETY PRECAUTIONS COMMON IN THE STATES. (OUTSIDE OF FTZs, AT LEAST.)

Phnom Penh International Airport

Canadia Industrial Park

VENG SRENG BLVD

SOME EVEN SIT ON SIMILARLY DENATIONALIZED TERRITORIES CALLED "SPECIAL ECONOMIC ZONES" THAT, LIKE FTZs, ALLOW FOR SUSPENSION OF LABOR LAWS AND HUMAN RIGHTS CONCERNS.

BETTER WORK HAITI'S (7) RECENT ANNUAL REPORT FOUND THAT 9% OF FACTORIES SURVEYED DID NOT COMPLY WITH REGULAR WORKING HOURS REGULATIONS AND HALF FAILED TO COMPLY WITH OVERTIME POLICIES. NO FACTORIES FULLY COMPLIED WITH MINIMUM WAGE LAWS, NEITHER DID ANY FACTORIES OFFER REQUIRED HEALTH AND FIRST AID SERVICES, WHILE MOST (83%) HAD IMPROPER EMERGENCY FACILITIES AND THE SAME NUMBER DID NOT TREAT CHEMICALS OR HAZARDOUS SUBSTANCES SAFELY. (8)

IN 2013, BETTER FACTORIES CAMBODIA FOUND 73% OF FACTORIES WITH EXCESSIVE HEAT LEVELS AND 61% LACKING SUFFICIENT CUPS FOR DRINKING WATER—AND WORKERS ARE OFTEN FIRED FOR FAINTING ON THE JOB. ADDITIONALLY, 2% OF THE FACTORIES HAD SUSPECTED CHILD LABORERS AND 16% ENGAGED IN SOME FORM OF DISCRIMINATION. (9)

ON JANUARY 3rd, 2014, AT LEAST 5 GARMENT WORKERS WERE KILLED, 40 WOUNDED, AND 10 ARRESTED AFTER MILITARY POLICE OPENED FIRE ON A DEMONSTRATION IN THE CANADIA INDUSTRIAL PARK, A SPECIAL ECONOMIC ZONE IN CAMBODIA. THE SHOOTINGS CAME AFTER SEVERAL DAYS OF STRIKES DEMANDING THE PRIME MINISTER STEP DOWN AND THE MINIMUM WAGE BE RAISED. NO ONE HAS YET BEEN HELD ACCOUNTABLE.

A 2013 SURVEY OF FACTORIES RELEASED BY THE BANGLADESH UNIVERSITY OF ENGINEERING AND TECHNOLOGY FOUND THAT 60% OF ALL FACTORIES IN BANGLADESH WERE STRUCTURALLY UNSOUND. (10)

IN DECEMBER 2013, THE OWNERS OF TAZREEN FASHIONS AND FOUR COMPANY OFFICIALS WERE CHARGED WITH HOMICIDE FOR THEIR PART IN THE DEATHS OF 112 WORKERS. THEY COULD FACE THE DEATH PENALTY.

It's The Money, Honey

Written by Anne Elizabeth Moore
Illustrated by Ellen Lindner

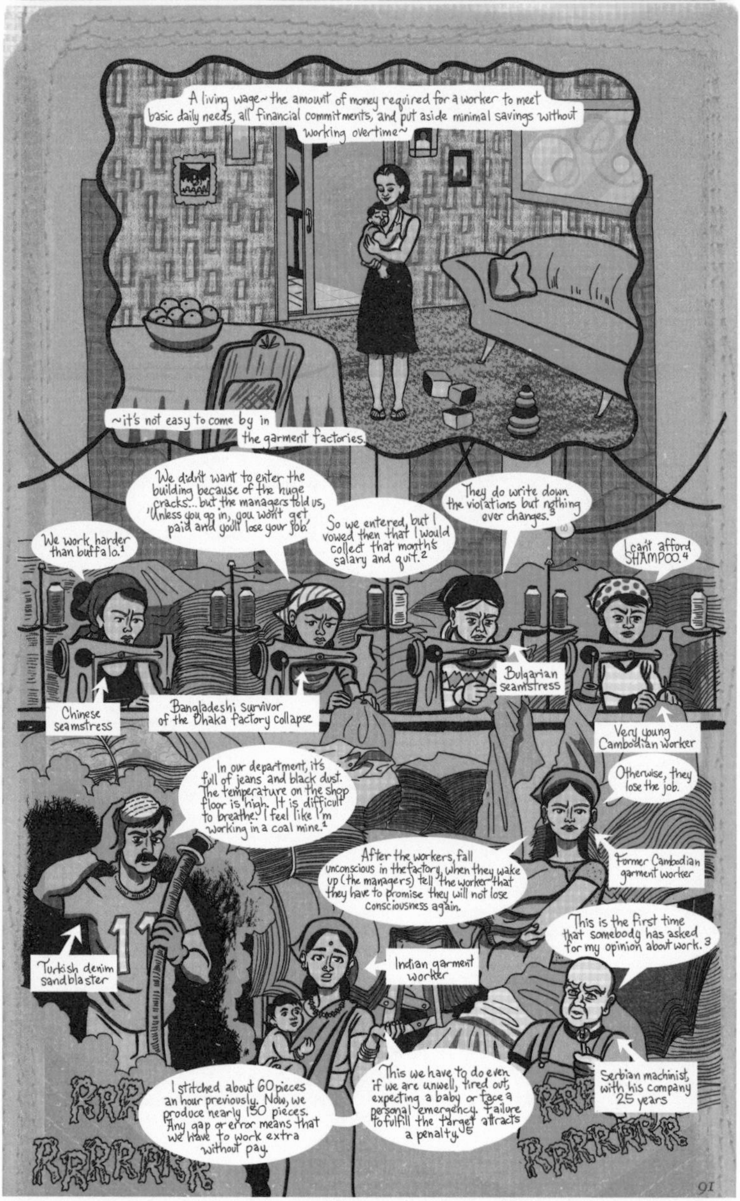
A living wage~ the amount of money required for a worker to meet basic daily needs, all financial commitments, and put aside minimal savings without working overtime~
~it's not easy to come by in the garment factories.
We work harder than buffalo.[1]
We didn't want to enter the building because of the huge cracks... but the managers told us, 'Unless you go in, you won't get paid and you'll lose your job.'
So we entered, but I vowed then that I would collect that month's salary and quit.[2]
They do write down the violations but nothing ever changes.[3]
I can't afford SHAMPOO.[4]
Chinese seamstress
Bangladeshi survivor of the Dhaka factory collapse
Bulgarian seamstress
Very young Cambodian worker
In our department, it's full of jeans and black dust. The temperature on the shop floor is high. It is difficult to breathe. I feel like I'm working in a coal mine.[1]
Otherwise, they lose the job.
After the workers fall unconscious in the factory, when they wake up (the managers) tell the worker that they have to promise they will not lose consciousness again.
Former Cambodian garment worker
This is the first time that somebody has asked for my opinion about work.[3]
Turkish denim sandblaster
Indian garment worker
I stitched about 60 pieces an hour previously. Now, we produce nearly 150 pieces. Any gap or error means that we have to work extra without pay.
This we have to do even if we are unwell, tired out, expecting a baby or face a personal emergency. Failure to fulfill the target attracts a penalty.[5]
Serbian machinist, with his company 25 years
RRR
RRRRRRR
RRR
RRRRRRR

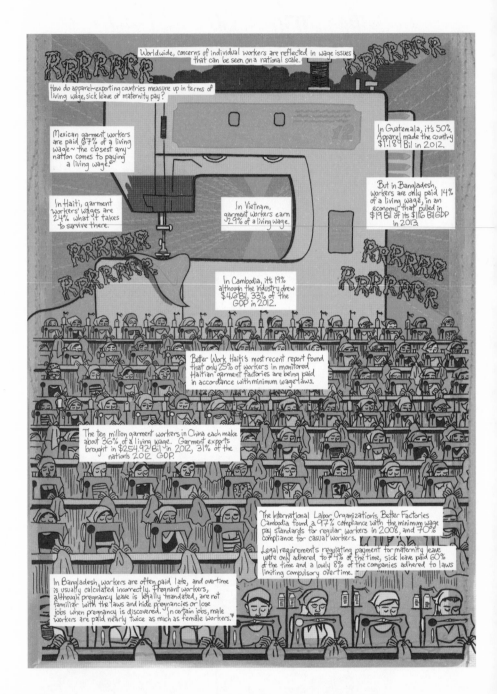

Worldwide, concerns of individual workers are reflected in wage issues that can be seen on a national scale.

How do apparel-exporting countries measure up in terms of living wage, sick leave or maternity pay?

Mexican garment workers are paid 67% of a living wage — the closest any nation comes to paying a living wage.

In Guatemala, it's 50%. Apparel made the country $1.189 Bil in 2012.

In Haiti, garment workers' wages are 24% what it takes to survive there.

In Vietnam, garment workers earn 29% of a living wage.

But in Bangladesh, workers are only paid 14% of a living wage, in an economy that pulled in $19 Bil of its $116 Bil GDP in 2013.

In Cambodia, it's 19% although the industry drew $4.6 Bil, 33% of the GDP in 2012.

Better Work Haiti's most recent report found that only 25% of workers in monitored Haitian garment factories are being paid in accordance with minimum wage laws.

The ten million garment workers in China each make about 36% of a living wage. Garment exports brought in $254.92 Bil in 2012, 31% of the nation's 2012 GDP.

The International Labor Organization's Better Factories Cambodia found a 97% compliance with the minimum wage pay standards for regular workers in 2008, and 70% compliance for casual workers.

Legal requirements regulating payment for maternity leave were only adhered to 74% of the time, sick leave paid 60% of the time and a lowly 8% of the companies adhered to laws limiting compulsory overtime.

In Bangladesh, workers are often paid late, and overtime is usually calculated incorrectly. Pregnant workers, although pregnancy leave is legally mandated, are not familiar with the laws and hide pregnancies or lose jobs when pregnancy is discovered. In certain jobs, male workers are paid nearly twice as much as female workers.

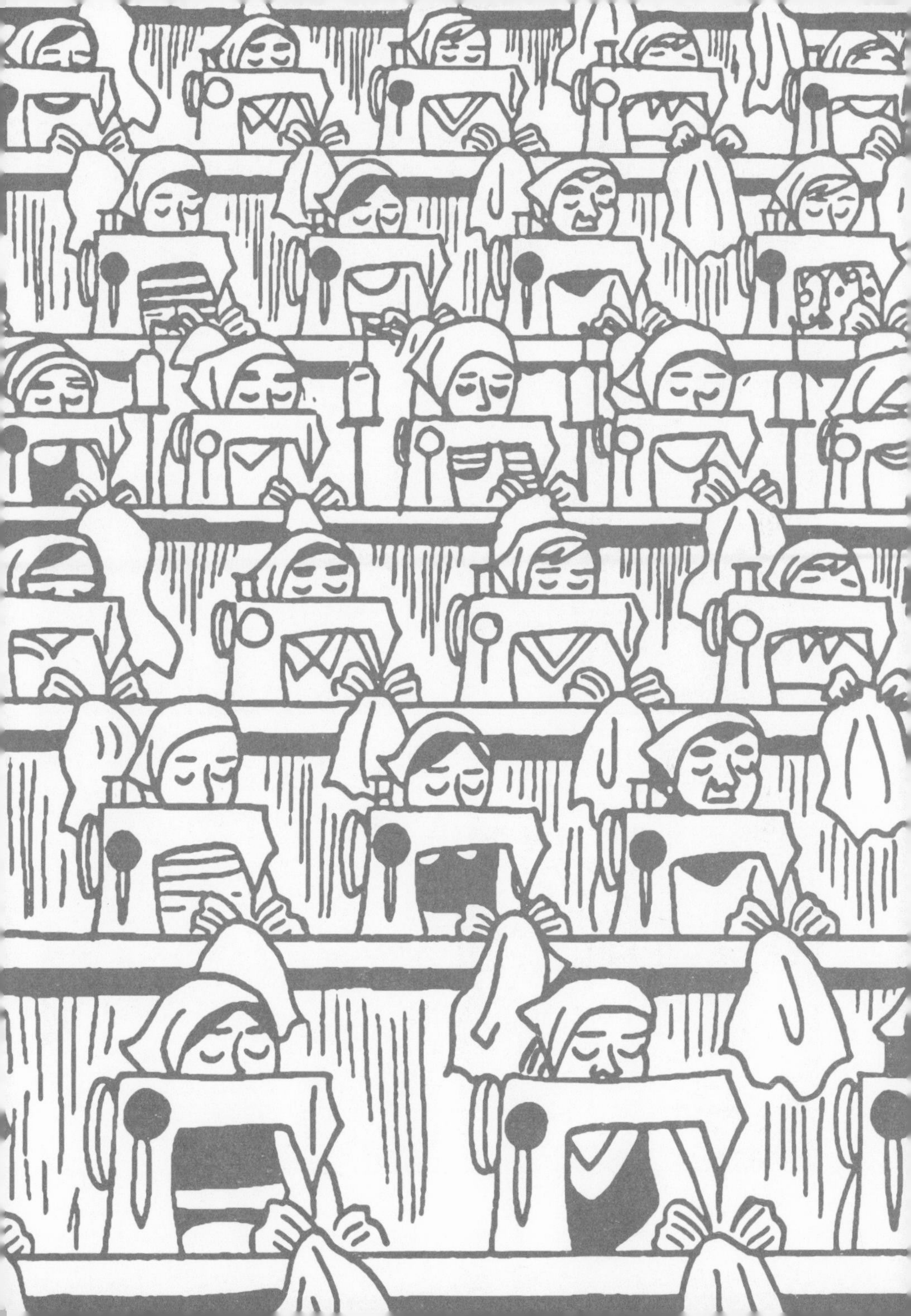

OUT OF THE FACTORIES

Words by Anne Elizabeth Moore   Pictures by Ellen Lindner   Additional research by Melissa Gira Grant

Phnom Penh, Cambodia~ January 2014

I'm going to tell you the rules real quick.

I'm visiting an anti~sex trafficking NGO that seeks to "eradicate enslavement" in the sex industry by offering alternative "fair trade" employment opportunities.[1]

We don't allow photography.

Of course.

I might tell you a client's testimony, but I will be sure to leave out any identifying information. We ask that you refrain from asking our clients about their past lives in the sex industry, because that causes them shame.

So how do journalists usually verify the stories they hear here?

I guess it's a matter of trust. All of our clients' stories come through interviews with our trained social workers. You could talk with one of them, if you wanted to confirm. But we don't want to put our customers through that.

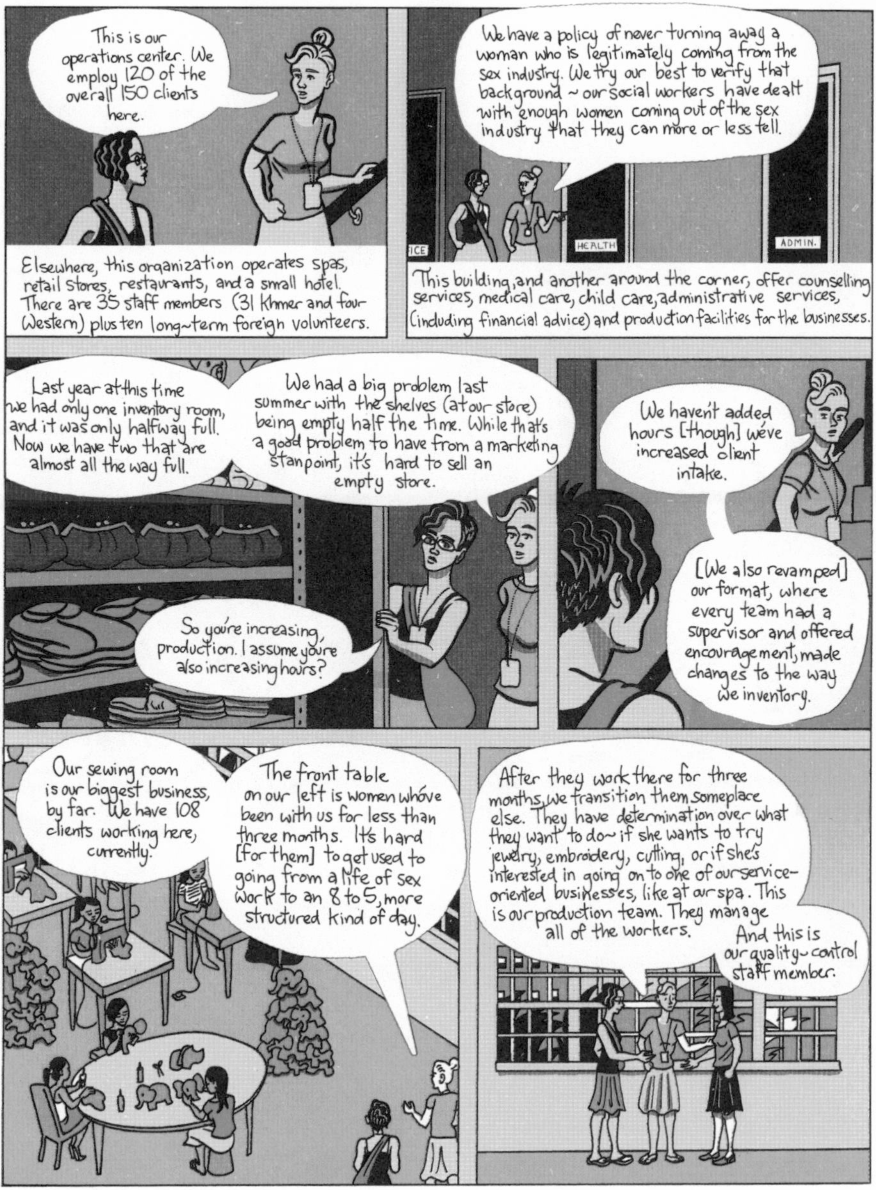
This is our operations center. We employ 120 of the overall 150 clients here.
Elsewhere, this organization operates spas, retail stores, restaurants, and a small hotel. There are 35 staff members (31 Khmer and four Western) plus ten long~term foreign volunteers.
We have a policy of never turning away a woman who is legitimately coming from the sex industry. We try our best to verify that background ~ our social workers have dealt with enough women coming out of the sex industry that they can more or less tell.
ICE
HEALTH
ADMIN.
This building, and another around the corner, offer counselling services, medical care, child care, administrative services, (including financial advice) and production facilities for the businesses.
Last year at this time we had only one inventory room, and it was only halfway full. Now we have two that are almost all the way full.
We had a big problem last summer with the shelves (at our store) being empty half the time. While that's a good problem to have from a marketing stanpoint, it's hard to sell an empty store.
So you're increasing production. I assume you're also increasing hours?
We haven't added hours [though] we've increased client intake.
[We also revamped] our format, where every team had a supervisor and offered encouragement, made changes to the way we inventory.
Our sewing room is our biggest business, by far. We have 108 clients working here, currently.
The front table on our left is women who've been with us for less than three months. It's hard [for them] to get used to going from a life of sex work to an 8 to 5, more structured kind of day.
After they work there for three months, we transition them someplace else. They have determination over what they want to do~ if she wants to try jewelry, embroidery, cutting, or if she's interested in going on to one of our service-oriented businesses, like at our spa. This is our production team. They manage all of the workers.
And this is our quality~control staff member.

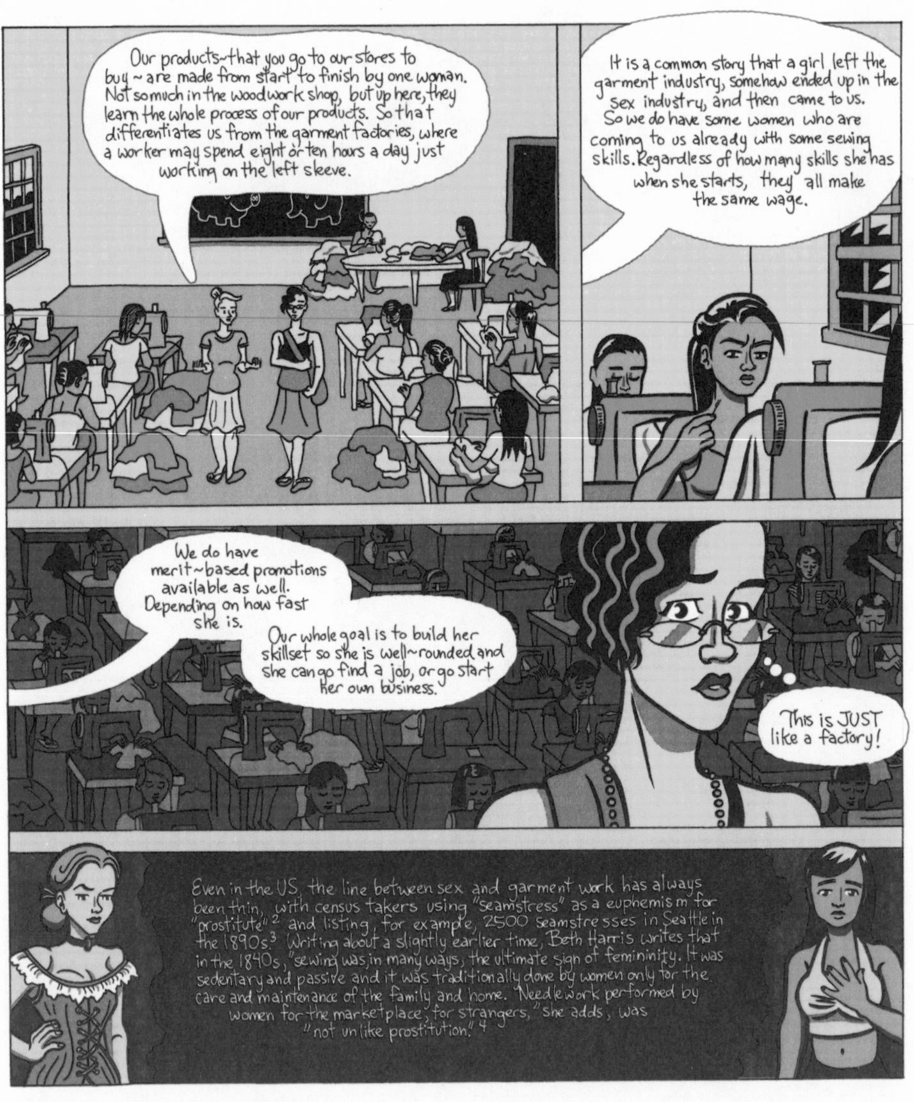
Our products~that you go to our stores to buy ~ are made from start to finish by one woman. Not so much in the woodwork shop, but up here, they learn the whole process of our products. So that differentiates us from the garment factories, where a worker may spend eight or ten hours a day just working on the left sleeve.
It is a common story that a girl left the garment industry, somehow ended up in the sex industry, and then came to us. So we do have some women who are coming to us already with some sewing skills. Regardless of how many skills she has when she starts, they all make the same wage.
We do have merit~based promotions available as well. Depending on how fast she is.
Our whole goal is to build her skillset so she is well~rounded and she can go find a job, or go start her own business.
This is JUST like a factory!
Even in the US, the line between sex and garment work has always been thin, with census takers using "seamstress" as a euphemism for "prostitute"[2] and listing, for example, 2500 seamstresses in Seattle in the 1890s.[3] Writing about a slightly earlier time, Beth Harris writes that in the 1840s, "sewing was, in many ways, the ultimate sign of femininity. It was sedentary and passive and it was traditionally done by women only for the care and maintenance of the family and home. Needlework performed by women for the marketplace, for strangers," she adds, was "not unlike prostitution."[4]

OUT of the FACTORIES Part 2

Words by Anne Elizabeth Moore
Pictures by Ellen Lindner

We're at an NGO in a so-called "red light district" of Phnom Penh, Cambodia~a place where most women have only two options to support families...

...sex work or garment work.

It was founded in 2007 by a psychologist from the UK who'd noticed, while working at other anti~trafficking organizations, that women who came to NGOs to leave sex work often went right back home again later...

...which resulted in her being re~trafficked.

One of the keys to keeping women out of the sex industry is the provision of that income to meet the financial demands of the family.

Income-generation work is anti~trafficking work, because when that family has a huge financial need, they're going to traffick their daughter.

So women come to us, they work for us, and we pay them an income just like any other job.

All of the training that they do, any of the counselling they get, and extracurricular education they receive, that's still paid time on the clock.

It's part of their job with us.

BRINGRDINGBRING

In Cambodia, community is very important, even if that community is sex workers.

Central to this NGO's mission is that women remain in their own homes~this isn't a shelter.

But somehow, the import granted clients' community doesn't always translate into respect for its needs.

We have one girl who had been sold against her will, in a brothel, by a pimp...

There was a police raid on her brothel, and she was brought to a shelter.

She said she HATED it.

She said...

There was a gate with razor~wire.

...and after three nights, my pimp came and rescued me.

The door was locked; I cried myself to sleep, every night...

So her pimp coming and returning her to sexual exploitation at that point was better than the shelter.

This NGO has clients retaining their own social safety nets while acquiring income from an alternative source...

There are definitely challenges to having women work in a community where there are still many sex workers and still many pimps~ but there are also a lot of advantages.

Nationally, how big of an impact do you think you have?

...although it does nothing to address the national social and economic factors and international trade policies that keep options for women limited in Cambodia.

That's very difficult to measure. I've read studies that say there are 15,000 prostitutes in Cambodia and others that say there are 50,000. I can tell you that most of our clients come from this geographical area: a low-income district on the eastern edge of the city.

Women who live here tend to service local Cambodian men, who make up the bulk of clients in the Cambodian sex industry.[1]

Those are the women whose salaries we can compete with~ a woman working on the riverside might make $20 per night from Westerners. Unless she really wants to leave the sex industry, we just can't compete with that.

What kinds of incomes are you needing to compete with here?

It depends on how many men she's seeing per night, and what her standard of beauty is considered to be, but hereabouts you could buy sex for less than $5 per night. How much of that the woman is making after the karaoke bar owner takes a cut or the hostess bar owner or the pimp takes a cut~it could be maybe $2.

Cambodian wages

Garment workers: $100 per month before overtime

High school teachers: $85~100 per month before bribes

Elementary school teachers: $50~$70 before bribes.[2]

Laborers at a local private university: $60 per month.

Grocery store clerks: $60 per month.

Food vendors: $75~$150 per month

Hostess bars typically pay women between $50 and $60 per month (before their cut of tips and "lady drinks", which are beverages purchased by customers that give them a dollar or two profit.)

By comparison, tuk-tuk drivers, another informal job like food vending and sex work, make $100~250 per month, although this is not a job traditionally held by women.[3]

So are you aiming to provide $2 per day, or $5 per day?

We do try to compete with $2 per day, but one of our biggest selling points is that we compete in other ways. We have free childcare, free education, free English education, which a lot of women are interested in, free medical care, and an abuse-free environment.

Some of the women do take a pay cut to work with us.

Living wage in Cambodia for single-earner households is about $150 per month.[4]

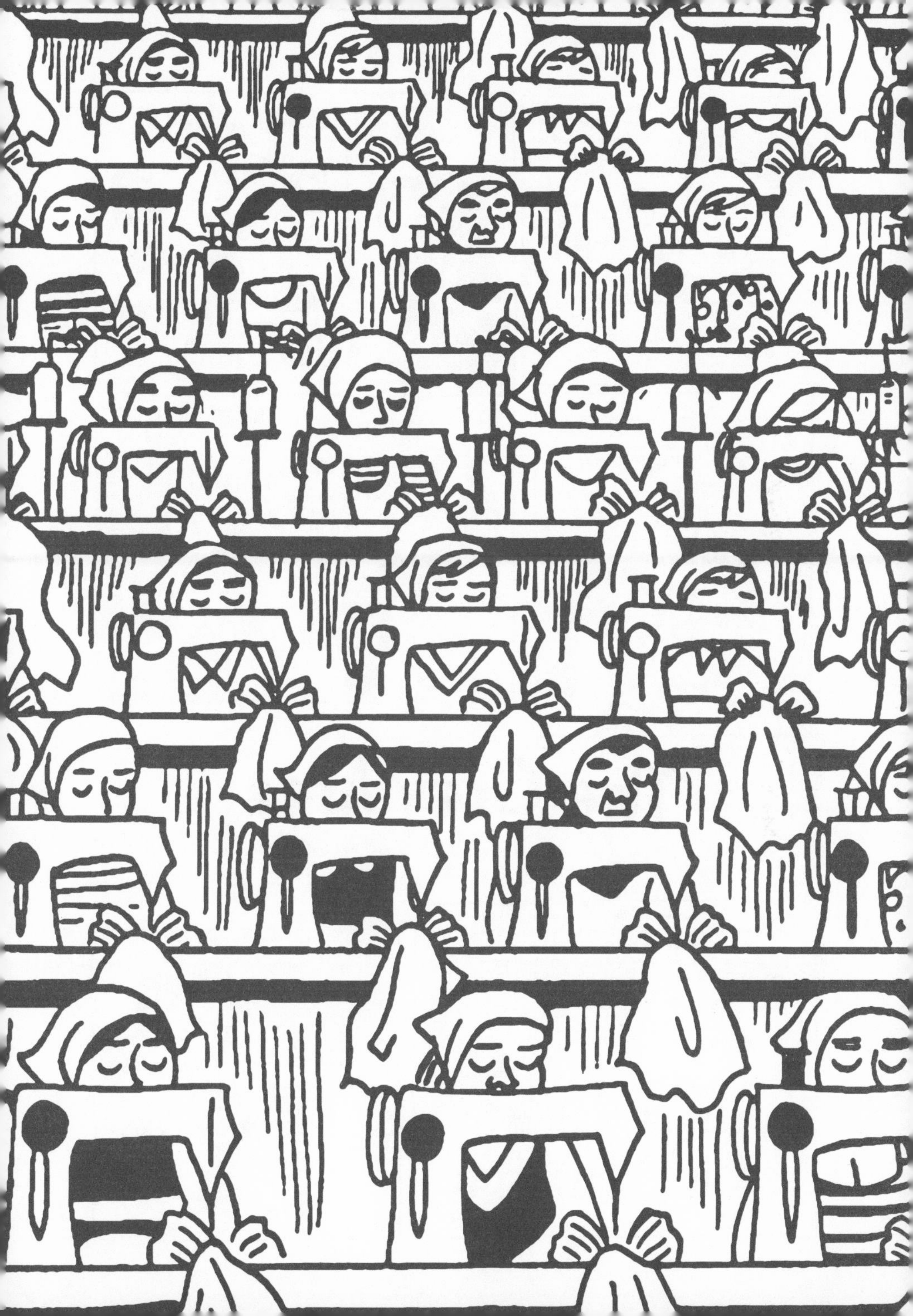

One of the problems with anti-trafficking organizations is that no one really seems to know what "trafficking" is.

Trafficking would be, when a woman is sold against her will. Someone who is sold, at least initially. We do have women here who — most of them were sold, or at least put under a lot of pressure from their families, to go into the sex industry themselves. (1)

"It does blur because there are women who say, 'My mom got really sick and we didn't have anyone to pay her bills, so I decided that I was going to traffic myself.'"

It's terms like "traffic myself" that generate a lot of confusion. If trafficking means a loss of agency, one can't traffic oneself.

"Then we have some who say, 'My aunt told me she get me a job as a domestic servant, and the next thing I knew I was being dropped off at a brothel or karaoke bar and being told that that's where I worked now.'"

"So you get both, and then you also get things

where things aren't so clear, where the family is pushing and pushing this girl, saying, You have to make money for us.

"There's definitely a line that gets blurry. We also have a lot of women who maybe crossed that line.

Maybe they were initially sold against their will a lot of times sold as underage girls, but then there came a point where they didn't owe a debt to the brothel owner anymore, and they continued working as sex workers.

So they aren't being held in chains... but they are being entrapped by lack of other alternatives, and the fact that there's still pressure on them from their families to generate an income."

The Grey Area

WRITTEN BY ANNE ELIZABETH MOORE
DRAWN BY LEELA CORMAN

The problem is: the lack of other alternatives is the issue. Cambodian tradition, history, and sensibility demand a daughter will do what she can to take care of her family. But as we have seen, the local economy offers women very few ways to do that. Which allows an NGO to claim...

"Income-generation work is anti-trafficking work, because when that family has a huge financial need, they're going to traffic their daughter."

DON'T TALK TO ME ABOUT SEWING MACHINES TALK TO ME ABOUT WORKERS' RIGHTS (2)

... even though it normalizes the egregious labor practices in developing nations that are standard in the apparel industry. But of course...

"It's exciting to think that women in the sex industry are forced into sexual bondage by evil men, but the boring reality is that most often we have to go to work to pay the bills, just like everyone else. (3)

Normalizing the lopsided economic gains in the apparel trade ensures a client base for anti-human trafficking NGOs—women who can't take the low wages, bad conditions, and monotonous work of the garment industry and leave it for the sex trade.

"We have an outreach program."

In nearby Laos, an AFESIP researcher asked twelve women working in beer halls and also selling sex why they had left garment work. Five said they needed more money; four said they were bored with apparel; and three said disputes with managers in the factories had forced their exit. (4)

"Actually since we restarted our outreach program last fall, new client intake increased around 35%."

That NGOs can be run like factories isn't surprising. But their concern for individual agency and autonomy doesn't always square with its treatment of workers.

We were one of the first organizations to work with transgender sex workers, so men who dress as women and sell their bodies to male clients.

So people who identify as women?

Well, none of them have undergone any kind of operation. There's a lot of grey area.

There really isn't. Trans rights organizations agree that ignoring the gender identity and pronoun choices of an individual is shaming if not psychologically abusive. This is particularly significant, given studies that show transgender sex workers to be at greater risk of harassment, abuse and rape — especially in Southeast Asia.

Love 146, an organization with the stated mission to abolish child trafficking and exploitation, found that 39% of Cambodian transwomen sex workers reported sexual or physical abuse at the hands of police.

"In Thailand, 'ladyboys' are more culturally accepted. Cambodia is more culturally conservative. Some of them have been kicked out by their families. Most of them can't find work because no one wants to employ them because of their appearance. So a lot of times, sex work is something they turn to just to put food in their belly or a roof over their heads."

But Love 146 (who is one of the funders of this Phnom Penh-based anti-trafficking NGO) also refers to transwomen as "transgendered males." (5)

So anti-trafficking NGOs are not only confused about what "trafficking" is; they're also confused about their own clients' preferred pronouns and gender identities.

Can we really trust them to provide reliable data on who they're "rescuing" and from what? (Especially if reporters are only granted access if they agree not to verify stories independently?)

Endnotes for Chapter Three

Outta Sight! (Outta Mind)

1. "Avoiding the fire next time," *The Economist* (May 4 2013). http://www.economist.com/news/business/21577078-after-dhaka-factory-collapse-foreign-clothing-firms-are-under-pressure-improve-working (accessed September 23, 2015).

2. Shelly Banjo and Syed Zain Al-Mahmood. "Bangladeshi garment exports surge despite dccidents," *Wall Street Journal* (Oct. 10, 2013). http://www.wsj.com/articles/SB10001424052702304500404579127314213623956 (accessed September 23, 2015).

3. *The Observatory of Economic Complexity: Haiti*, Massachussetts Institute of Technology. http://atlas.media.mit.edu/country/hti/ (accessed Dec. 30, 2013).

4. *CIA World Factbook*. 2012. "Haiti." Https://www.cia.gov/library/publications/the-world-factbook/geos/ha.html (accessed Dec. 30, 2013).

5. *Women's Participation in Trade Unions in Bangladesh*, Bangladesh Institute of Labor Studies, Dhaka (August 2009). http://www.ilo.org/wcmsp5/groups/public/@asia/@ro-bangkok/@ilo-dhaka/documents/publication/wcms_125374.pdf (accessed September 23, 2015).

6. If that seems high, note that there are occasionally two competing unions from the same federation in the same factory, which cuts effectiveness significantly, and "yellow unions"—started by management—have also been reported. See *Women and Gender Issues in Trade Unions in the Cambodian Garment Industry*, ILO's Social Protection and Gender Project, by Veasna Nuon et. al, (2011).

7. The Better Factories programs are monitoring organizations of the ILO. While they did groundbreaking work when they started in Cambodia in the mid-1990s, they have more recently come under criticism for lack of effectiveness and disinterest in addressing wage issues.

8. *Garment Industry 7th Biannual Synthesis Report Under the HOPE II Legislation,* Better Work Haiti, The International Labour Organization (Oct. 16 2013). http://betterwork.org/global/wp-content/uploads/HOPE-II-FINAL_merged1.pdf (accessed September 23, 2015).

9. *Thirtieth Synthesis Report on Working Condititions in Cambodia's Garment Sector,* Better Factories Cambodia, The International Labour Organization (July 18 2013).

10. Jason Burke. "Majority of Bangladesh garment factories vulnerable to collapse." *The Guardian* (June 3, 2013). http://www.theguardian.com/world/2013/jun/03/bangladesh-garment-factories-vulnerable-collapse (accessed September 23, 2015).

It's the Money, Honey

1. *Breathless for Blue Jeans,* Clean Clothes Campaign, June 2013. http://www.cleanclothes.org/resources/publications/Breathless-Exec-Summary (accessed September 23, 2015).

2. Julie McCarthy, "Bangladesh collapse: The garment workers who survived," *NPR's Marketplace,* July 10, 2013. http://www.npr.org/sections/parallels/2013/07/10/200644781/Bangladesh-Collapse-The-Garment-Workers-Who-Survived (accessed September 23, 2015).

3. *Worker's Voices,* Clean Clothes Campaign, 2005. http://www.cleanclothes.org/resources/national-cccs/05-workers-voices.pdf (accessed September 23, 2015).

4. Personal interviews, 2010-2014.

5. "India—women garment industry workers," *Pushpa Achanta,* Women's UN Report Network, March 13, 2013. Http://www.wunrn.com/news/2013/05_13/05_13/051313_india.htm (accessed September 23, 2015).

6. All living wage figures from 2011, cited in a 2013 report, *Global Wage Trends for Apparel Workers 2001-2011,* from the Center for American Progress. These countries

are among the top 20 that export clothes to the U.S. annually. Download the report at https://www.americanprogress.org/issues/labor/report/2013/07/11/69255/global-wage-trends-for-apparel-workers-2001-2011/ (accessed September 23, 2015).

7. Ferdous Ahamed. "Improving social compliance in Bangladesh's ready-made garment industry," *Labor and Management in Development*, Vol. 3. http://www.nla.gov.au/openpublish/index.php/lmd/article/viewFile/2269/3148 (accessed February 20, 2014).

Out of the Factories, Part I

1. Via the organization's website. Because I don't believe this organization is worthy of either praise or ridicule—and neither was my guide for the day—they will remain anonymous. (Dialogue from a tape-recorded tour of the facility.)

2. Jeff Foret, *Race Relations at the Margins* (Louisiana State University Press, 2006). P. 202.

3. Ken Van Vechten. "History Hidden in Seattle's Basement," *Los Angeles Times*, November 13, 2011.

4. Beth Harris, "Slaves of the Needle." http://www.victorianweb.org/gender/ugoretz1.html (accessed March 14, 2014).

Out of the Factories, Part II

1. Most studies estimate that Cambodian men make up 50%-70% of the client base for sex workers, with other Asian sex tourists making up the second-largest part, and European and American men only making up a single-digit percentage of clientele.

2. Teachers and government employees are often paid late if at all, and many charge students fees (thank-you money) that they use to buy food. Garment workers' sala-

ries fluctuate based on overtime hours, which are often mandatory.

3. Based on personal interviews conducted January 2014.

4. In February 2009, the Cambodia Institute of Development Study collected the actual costs accrued by a survey of 353 garment workers, and reported that the minimum living wage was $90 five years ago and the maximum $120. Based on projected cost-of-living increases, we can estimate a current minimum living wage of $113 for women in Cambodia contributing equal amounts to family income alongside others, a position women in the sex industry do not tend to hold.

The Grey Area

1. All quotes otherwise unattributed are from a personal interview at an anti human-trafficking NGO in Phnom Penh, Cambodia in January, 2014.

2. Inspired by a sign made by the Asia Pacific Network of Sex Workers, photograph by Melissa Gira Grant. http://www.flickr.com/photos/melissagira/447953273/ (accessed April 22, 2014).

3. Tara Burns, "Are You Being Sex Trafficked?" *The New Inquiry.* http://thenewinquiry.com/features/are-you-being-sex-trafficked/ (accessed April 22, 2014).

4. AFESIP (Agir pour les Femmes en Situation Precaire, most commonly translated from the French as "Women in Distressing Situations") is the anti-sex trafficking organization founded in 1996 by the controversial Somaly Mam. "The transition of garment factory girls into prostitution in Laos," Geneva Switzerland, 2007, p. 21. http://www.afesiplaos.org/upload/assets/OS_Garment%20factory%20girls_06.pdf (accessed April 28, 2014).

5. The preferred term is "transgender," as it is less totalizing than the past participle "transgendered." http://prezi.com/qlftfijogf5d/ (accessed April 22, 2014).

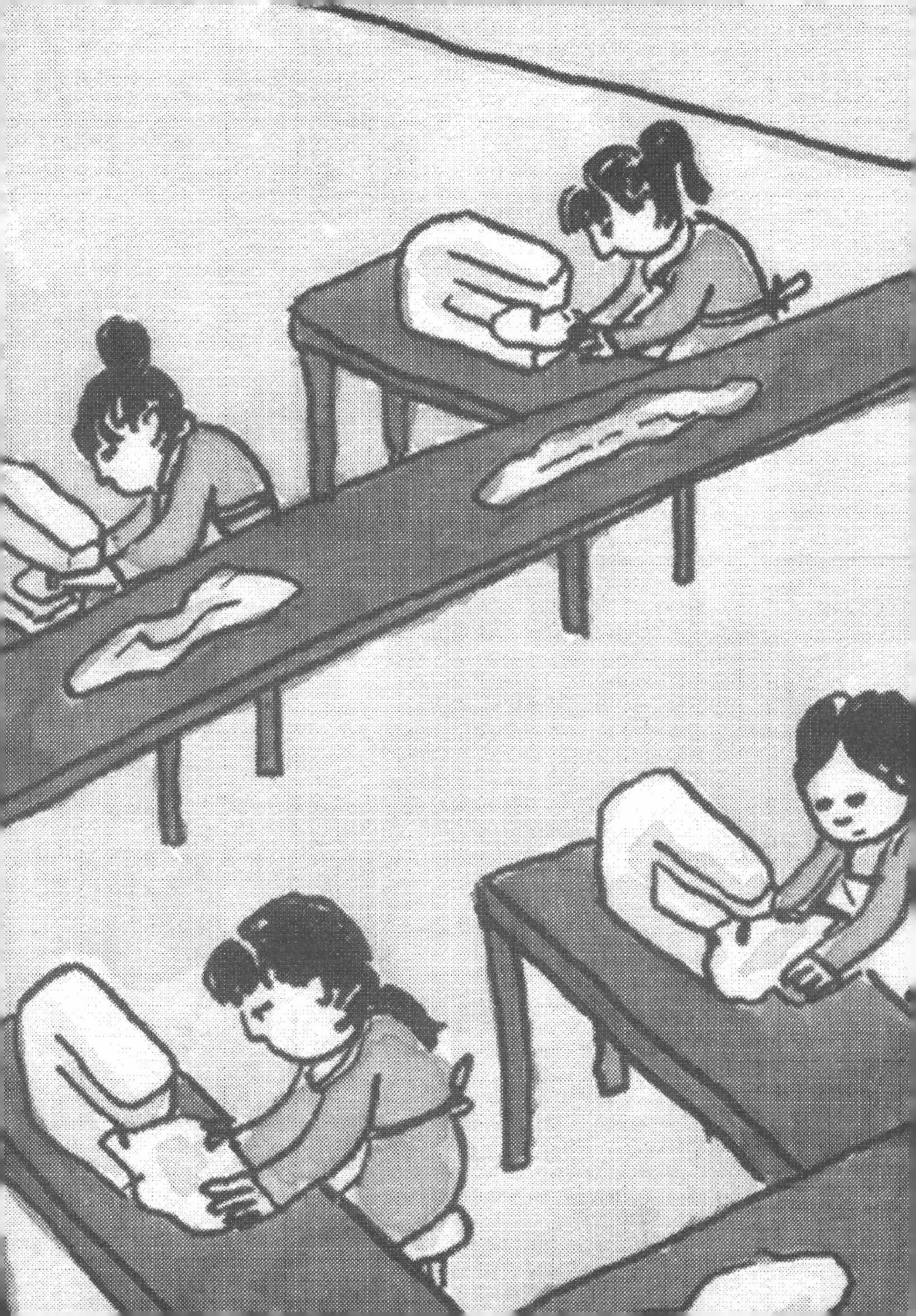

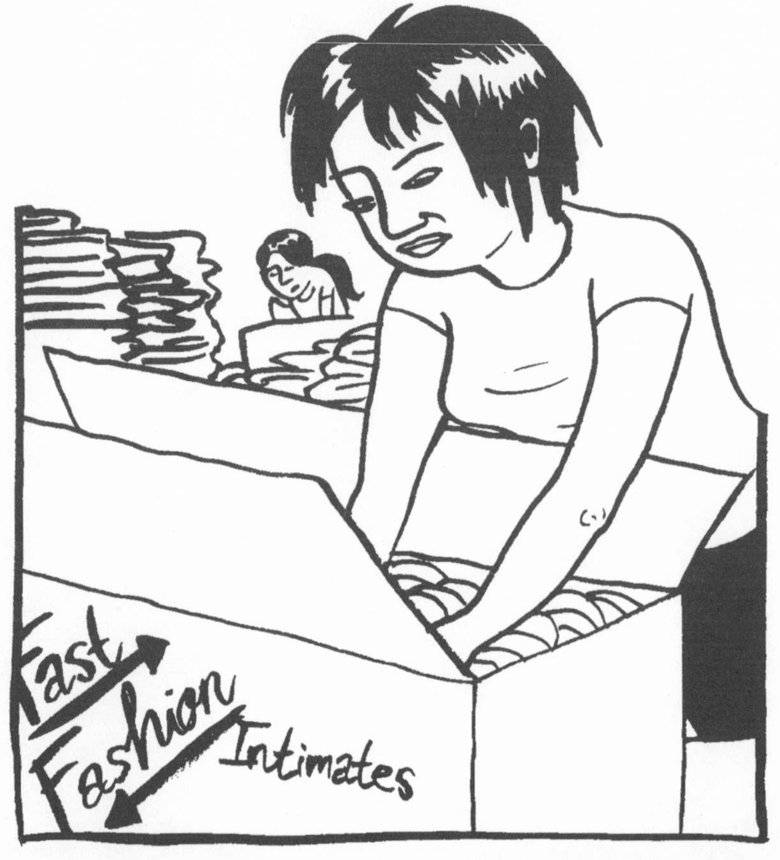
Fast Fashion
Intimates

Chapter 4 : The World

By now it will be clear that the globalization of the garment industry means that the precise locations of these incidents matters very little. It is unfortunately true that labor and human rights abuses take place at every stop on the production and distribution line. A Bangladesh garment factory building collapse echoes the Triangle Shirtwaist Factory Fire in the U.S. a century earlier. A Cambodian sex worker is jailed and placed in rehabilitation as a trafficking survivor just as an American one will be, or an Ecuadorian one, or a Chinese one, in the U.S. We're calling this chapter "The World," then, as shorthand for "how international policies created in the U.S. operate on the ground throughout the world, and then are repatriated and used to suppress women domestically, too."

Our narrative in this chapter starts with Somaly Mam, a self-proclaimed former victim of sex trafficking in Cambodia. Mam claims to have rescued more than 4,000 girls from sex slavery through her Cambodian NGO AFESIP and its global fundraising arm, the Somaly Mam Foundation. Mam's influence on U.S. policy-making is vast. She was named Glamour's "Woman of the Year" in 2006, a "Hero of Anti-Trafficking" by the U.S. State Department in 2007, and one of Time's "Most Influential People" in 2009.

Many of these accolades can be traced back to her friendship with New York *Times* columnist Nick Kristof, which only soured when a May 2014 Newsweek story debunked many of Mam's claims. Following up on several years' worth of investigative work by reporter Simon Marks, *Newsweek* outlined the many allegations of falsehoods in Mam's biography. These include her own childhood exploitation and accounts of her daughter's kidnapping by pro-trafficking thugs. Perhaps more important, a full accounting of Mam's falsehoods includes several stories told by survivors who lived in her facilities, who later say they were coached by Mam and staff with lurid tales of their harrowing escapes from brothels. The most renowned of these, Somana Pros (who met with Hillary Clinton and was featured on *Oprah*) has acted, since 2005, as an ardent and outspoken activist on sexual health and women's rights. She is featured prominently telling her own tale of rape and abuse at the hands of a pimp in Kristof's 2012 PBS series *Half the Sky*—she is missing an eye, and describes a brothel-owner stabbing it out—but a local paper dug up medical records that indicate she had had a tumor removed in 2005, right before Pros moved to Mam's facility.

Even Mam's saviorhood, however, is disputable. A January 2014 independent report from the Urban Institute found that only 49 percent of the 674 women and girls at AFESIP shelters between 2008 and 2012 could be considered "trafficked" under any definition of the term.

Unfortunately, these falsehoods have proven quite profitable, to Mam as well as to right-wing Christian fundamentalist NGOs, which have used the mantle of human trafficking to promote agendas that are clearly unrelated, such as abstinence education in U.S. schools and Christian religious instruction in Buddhist or Muslim areas abroad. And while Mam can't be held accountable for the impact of her tales, she can be taken to task for establishing the culture of permanent victimhood we grant to anti-trafficking NGO clients. When I entered my first human trafficking NGO, what I witnessed was not shocking: totally normal Cambodian women in a large room, sewing apparel. (I had witnessed similar scenes many times.) What was shocking was that I was not allowed to ask the women any questions about "their previous lives," a distinction that covered any question I might ask. I certainly wasn't going to ask if they were excited about the jobs they'd be placed in, in the low-paying, high-risk garment sector. Usually, an enforced culture of silence shrouds abuse and coercion. Yet somehow we've been given to believe—by Mam, Kristof and hand-selected victims who sometimes turn out, later, to have been fed scripted hard-luck tales—that here, silence is nothing but healing.

Corollary to this concern, that prizes the silencing of women, is that we are given to believe that freedom from oppression is easy. Ending deeply embedded misogynistic practices, including both sex trafficking (which is likely rarer than Mam admits) and the damaging policies supposedly waging war against it, is not an effortless gig. Both would be excellent projects, if we chose to take them on. Unfortunately, what anti-human trafficking NGOs really do is instead quite damaging: they normalize existent labor opportunities for women, no matter how low the pay, dangerous the conditions, or abusive an environment they foster. And they shame women who reject such jobs. The true impact of the U.S.-led human trafficking movement around the world is unfortunately bleak.

What anti-trafficking NGOs are saving women from, in other words, is a life outside the international garment trade—even though folks in the factories tell me they can barely survive. Around 350,000 people, 90 percent women, work in the garment industry in Cambodia, earning, as of late 2015, less than two-thirds of a living wage. About one seventh of the world's population of women works in the garment industry, which very rarely pays more than half a living wage (including to folks who work fast fashion retail in U.S. urban centers). This helps keep women in poverty around the globe.

In Cambodia, massive strikes in recent years have seen demand grow for an increase in pay—including the one that ended in violence in the Special Economic Zone outside of Phnom Penh—although other jobs for women remain few and unregulated. Work in the sex industry is both reliable and flexible enough for, say, working moms. Most women in Cambodia live under conditions of poverty and desperation, and the garment industry's refusal to meet living-wage standards ensures this will continue for some time. Still, garment workers know an entire international trade system relies on their willing participation, which was how they built such a strong showing in the last elections (and were able to rally the country to call for the prime minister to step down or pay them a decent wage). The big brands know how important workers are, too, which is why the Nike Foundation funds Half the Sky—as do other multinationals that both enforce and rely on women's desperate poverty around the world.

We call this "The Somaly Problem," the title of the Leela Corman strip that follows, which describes the wrong-headed idea that we can save women and girls by installing them in the garment industry—which really only perpetuates entrenched, gender-based poverty for generations.

It's a pretty big problem that Mam's helped bolster, but it's not an unsolvable one. Serpent Libertine, a sex worker and organizer with SWOP-Chicago, has seen the U.S. side of it up close, and helps us think through how Mam's influence on U.S. policy puts women workers in the U.S. in danger. Her argument, that human trafficking is only the latest moral panic, helps us consider what reasonable solutions there may be to limit the danger of our most vulnerable populations and ensure the human rights of women, around the world—even here in the U.S.

When anti-trafficking NGOs overlook the sexual agency and gender identity of their client population and prohibit journalists from verifying client stories,

we can be sure there's even more getting left out.

In May 2014, Cambodian anti-trafficking advocate Somaly Mam stepped down from her own foundation after a *Newsweek* story revealed she'd made misstatements(1) about her own history of sex trafficking and those of her clients.

Now Somaly seems like a sweet person, and clearly lied because she believed it would do more good than harm. But the stories she told, revealed as untruthful, fed a giant machine with an agenda she may not have seen.

The Somaly Problem

WRITTEN BY ANNE ELIZABETH MOORE
DRAWN BY LEELA CORMAN

Reporters like Nicholas Kristof presented Mam's stories as factual in the New York Times and his own documentary *Half the Sky*, bolstering his reputation with (and launching a foundation to support) women and girls, jailing some after brothel busts and posting pictures of others online without their permission. (2)

Celebrities like Angelina Jolie, Bono, and Mira Sorvino beat the youth-obsessed media culture and stagnating ticket sales by lending their recognizable faces to fundraising events for lascivious causes in the Global South.

Activists like Don Brewster, who founded Agape International Missions after a visit to a Cambodian village with a reputation for underage commercial sex, boosted his image (and probably his funding base) after a series of CNN reports glowingly covered his work — but failed to ask real questions about consensual sex work, gender-based oppression, or religious autonomy.

Don Brewster

Mira Sorvino

Among anti-traffickers, Christian ideals seem persistent. Love 146, that funds the NGO we visited in Phnom Penh, says that, while they're not a faith-based organization, they are "inspired by Christian faith." (3)

AIM boasts of conversion numbers among trafficking victims. (4)

"[Anti-trafficking NGOs] generally assume that trafficked persons need to be rescued — and, many times, need Jesus." (5)

Yvonne Zimmerman, professor of Christian Ethics and author of the 2012 book *Other Dreams of Freedom*, suggests that Bush's 2000 Trafficking Victims Prevention Act (TVPA), which uses positive and negative incentives to bolster anti-trafficking initiatives internationally, was founded on Protestant ideals like

Pious womanhood.

TVPA's "incentives" can lead to the cessation of US aid money for NGOs (or entire countries) that don't meet certain anti-trafficking benchmarks.

If you run an international NGO that relies on US money, you might feel forced to save a certain number of women from sex work to keep your organization running.

This may be why the numbers don't add up.

ESTIMATED HUMAN TRAFFICKING VICTIMS

CAMBODIA: 80,000–100,000

US: 15,000

WORLD: 2.4 MIL

DOCUMENTED HUMAN TRAFFICKING VICTIMS LAST YEAR

CAMBODIA: 1058

US: 238

WORLD: ??? (6)

But slippages like this lead to more, in the same way the impact of Mam's misstatements kept multiplying.

"I'm writing to ask for advice. I have been working with an anti-trafficking organization in India, where the director made personal use of donations and appears to have fabricated blah blah blah blah..."

The lies spread fast. Love146 claims to "serve children," but the 2012-13 Annual Report reveals a more complicated agenda.

Non-westerners, both youth and adults, made up only 44% of the clients served by their efforts. Of individuals, folks living in the US made up 56% of clients — most students in Connecticut or Boston. (7)

WAIT FOR THE BLING! VIRGIN: NOT A DIRTY WORD!

In other words, the majority of Love146's outreach isn't to potential victims of sex-trafficking.

It's to US-based participants in a word-of-mouth campaign to "spread awareness."

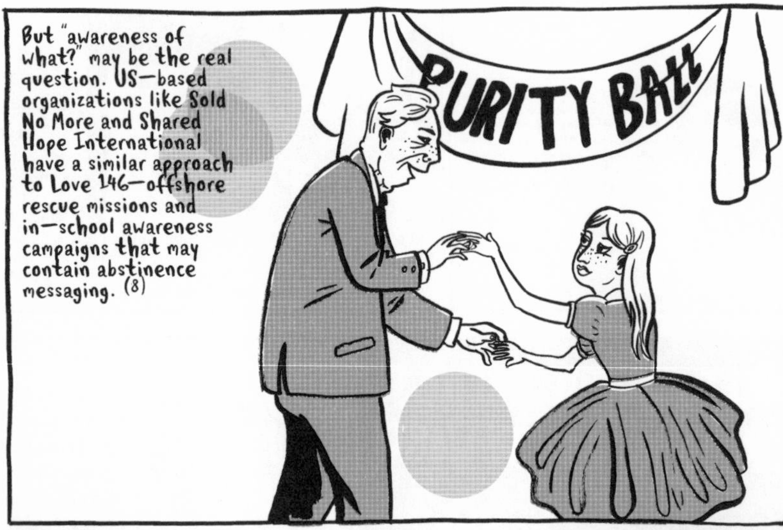
But "awareness of what?" may be the real question. US-based organizations like Sold No More and Shared Hope International have a similar approach to Love 146—offshore rescue missions and in-school awareness campaigns that may contain abstinence messaging. (8)
PURITY BALL

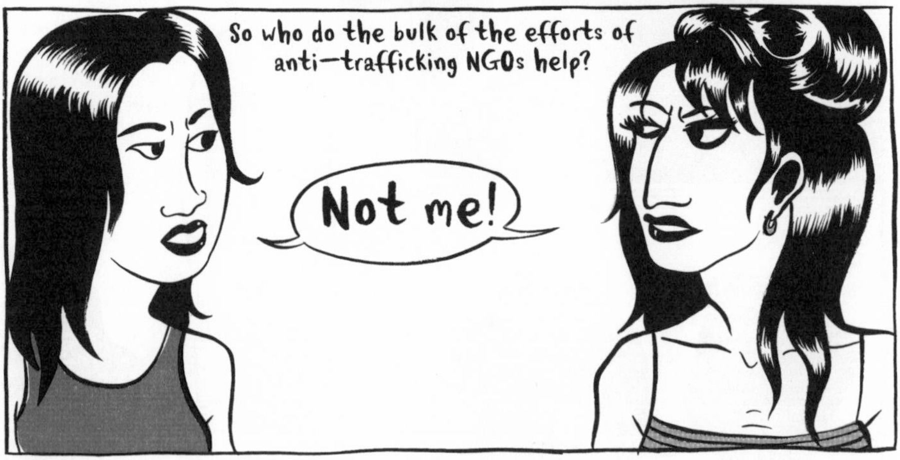
So who do the bulk of the efforts of anti-trafficking NGOs help?
Not me!

unraveling

written by
Anne Elizabeth Moore
drawn by
Melissa Mendes

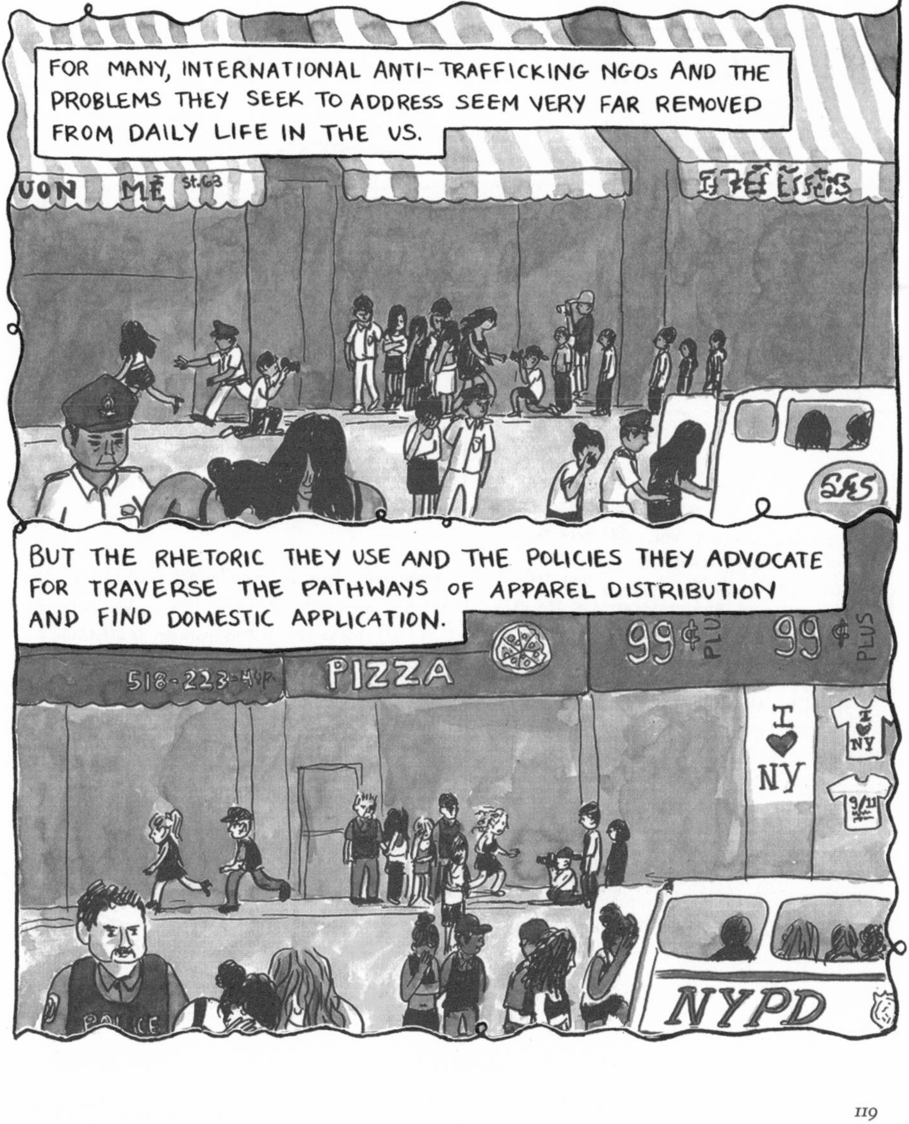
FOR MANY, INTERNATIONAL ANTI-TRAFFICKING NGOs AND THE PROBLEMS THEY SEEK TO ADDRESS SEEM VERY FAR REMOVED FROM DAILY LIFE IN THE US.
BUT THE RHETORIC THEY USE AND THE POLICIES THEY ADVOCATE FOR TRAVERSE THE PATHWAYS OF APPAREL DISTRIBUTION AND FIND DOMESTIC APPLICATION.
PIZZA
99¢ PLUS
99¢ PLUS
I ♥ NY
NYPD

IN JULY 2014, FOR EXAMPLE, THE FBI SHUT DOWN MYREDBOOK, A WEBSITE THAT OFFERED SEX WORKERS AFFORDABLE ACCESS TO CLIENT-VETTING TOOLS BLACKLISTED PATRONS, AND SAFETY RESOURCES.

"Almost all of the people who were involved in human trafficking were advertising their victims on MyRedBook." (1)

ALAMEDA COUNTY PROSECUTOR CASEY BATES TOLD *SFGATE* THAT WHILE THEY WEREN'T THE FOCUS OF THE EFFORT, CONSENSUAL SEX WORKERS MAKE UP A SLIM MINORITY OF THE PROSTITUTES WORKING IN THE BAY AREA. (2)

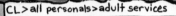

CL > all personals > adult services

reply

★hey honey

"The Internet has been identified as the number one platform that pimps, traffickers, and johns currently use for buying and selling women and children for sex in the United States," The Polaris Project, a US-focused anti-trafficking organization and political lobby explains. (3)

Similarly, the international NGO Coalition Against Trafficking in Women (CATW)–mission:"To end human trafficking in our lifetime"– advocates for laws that define all sex work as violence against women, and successfully campaigned to remove the "Adult Services" section from Craigslist. (4)

BUT THE INABILITY TO DISTINGUISH BETWEEN SEX WORK AND HUMAN TRAFFICKING DOES NOTHING TO CHANGE THE AVAILABLE OPPORTUNITIES FOR WOMEN TO MAKE A LIVING.

GIRLS

NOW HIRING

FOREVER 21°

HELP WANTED

WHICH MAY BE WHY THE GARMENT INDUSTRY IS SUCH A STRONG SUPPORTER OF ANTI-TRAFFICKING EFFORTS.

AFESIP.

$1.175 MIL BUDGET. (5)

CAMBODIAN NGO.

TRAINS FORMER TRAFFICKING VICTIMS IN APPAREL MANUFACTURING.

SUPPORTED BY AFESIP FAIR FASHION, A RETAIL OUTLET IN PHNOM PENH.

FOUNDED BY SOMALY MAM IN 1996, THE ORGANIZATION LET 39 STAFF MEMBERS GO IN 2014 WHEN THE SOMALY MAM FOUNDATION CUT FUNDING UNEXPECTEDLY.

THE SOMALY MAM FOUNDATION.

$2.8 MIL BUDGET.(6)

NEW YORK-BASED 501 (c)(3).

I love my work with Somaly. It fits in great with my position as VP of Global Sourcing for Gap Inc!

JANET RIVETT-CARNAC

FUNDED ORGANIZATIONS THAT TRAIN FORMER SEX TRAFFICKING VICTIMS IN APPAREL.

LISTED AS PARTNERS NO LESS THAN FIVE APPAREL AND MAKE UP OUTLETS OUT OF EIGHT TOTAL BEFORE SHUTTING DOWN IN 2014.

AGAPE INTERNATIONAL MISSIONS (AIM).

UNKNOWN BUDGET.

Hi, I'm Ken Peterson,

board member of Don Brewster's organization. I'm also the CEO of Apricot Lane, a fashion chain here in the US that carries all the big brands!

MANY OF THE BIG BRANDS THAT APRICOT LANE CARRIES ARE MANUFACTURED IN CHINA, SOUTH KOREA, AND PAKISTAN - PLACES KNOWN TO SUBCONTRACT WORK TO PLACES LIKE BANGLADESH AND CAMBODIA.

AIM IS ALSO SUPPORTED BY 3STRANDS, A JEWELRY STORE BY THE APRICOT LANE PEOPLE, AND AIM APPAREL AND AIM EMPLOYMENT CENTER, THAT OFFER CAREERS IN THE TEXTILE INDUSTRY.

INTERNATIONAL JUSTICE MISSION (IJM).

Hi, I'm Ram Gidoomal, board member of IJM. I also run a Christian-based fair-trade company and development charity called Traidcraft.

$47.95 MIL. (7)

IJM IS A 501(c)(3) BUT HAS SEVERAL INTERNATIONAL PARTNER ORGANIZATIONS REGISTERED IN THEIR OWN NATIONS.

SEVERAL STAFF AND BOARD MEMBERS HAVE GOVERNMENT CONNECTIONS.

THEY ALSO RECEIVE GOVERNMENT MONEY (ALTHOUGH DIFFERENT SOURCES PROVIDE DIFFERENT FIGURES)...

...AND LOBBY CONGRESS.

HALF THE SKY MOVEMENT.

THEIR FINANCIAL INFORMATION ISN'T AVAILABLE EITHER.

MAJOR DONORS INCLUDE THE NIKE FOUNDATION, FORMER PRESIDENT OF TIME'S STYLE AND ENTERTAINMENT GROUP FRAN HAUSER (NOW AN INVESTOR IN STARTUPS LIKE ZADY, WHICH BRANDS ITSELF AN ETHICAL FASHION COMPANY), AND IKEA—WHICH OF COURSE DOESN'T PRODUCE FAST FASHION. JUST WHERE WE STORE IT.

SOMALY MAM'S BEEN REMOVED FROM THE WEBSITE'S LIST OF "OTHER PARTNERS," BUT IJM, EQUALITY NOW, THE POLARIS PROJECT, AND SHARED HOPE INTERNATIONAL HAVEN'T.

SHARED HOPE INTERNATIONAL.

$3.4 MIL BUDGET. (8)

MAINTAINS A FOR-PROFIT ARM CALLED TRAFFICKING MARKETS, LLC.

WHICH SEEMS AN ODD THING FOR AN ORGANIZATION THAT SEEKS TO "PREVENT THE CONDITIONS THAT FOSTER SEX TRAFFICKING" TO DO. (9)

I'm Curtis Lind, here on behalf of Shared Hope International – but my day job's at Columbia Sportswear Company!

THE THREADS THAT CONNECT THE SEX INDUSTRY TO THE GARMENT INDUSTRY ARE MANY, ...

...BUT IF YOU LOOK CLOSELY, YOU CAN FIGURE OUT HOW TO UNRAVEL THEM.

Serpent Libertine

part I

When did this whole anti-trafficking thing even come about? When I started as a sex worker in the late 1990s, it wasn't on anybody's radar. (1)

Serpent Libertine is an organizer with the Sex Worker's Outreach Project in Chicago (SWOP-Chicago).

I did the [diversion program] Unhooked in 2003 when it was run by Genesis House, but I never heard the word "trafficking" when I went through that. That term was not being used at that time.

She's been in Chicago for over 15 years—doing sex work, organizing, and going to school—and may be the best person to explain what anti-trafficking legislation looks like, on the ground.

written by: ANNE ELIZABETH MOORE   drawn by: Delia Jean

Unhooked is a one-day program that you can go through after your first arrest and then you get your charges expunged. It's now run by Christian Community Health Center (CCHC).

Genesis House was good. They had housing. They did outreach to people in the sex trade, and they had a couple locations. The one I went to was on 55th and Ashland. For people who wanted to get out of the industry, they had a place to stay.

When you got arrested, you would go in and do a day-long group. The program has changed since I did it. It's now more structured. We kinda sat around in groups and talked about our feelings and then got a letter to give to the judge. Then they sent us off with a giant bag of candy.

CANDY sucke... A SSORT...

They assume everybody is a junkie and needs a sugar fix. The assumption is that folks aren't just getting unhooked from prostitution, but from drugs as well.

The women who ran Genesis House were getting Housing and Urban Development money and buying expensive cars and going on vacations. They got shut down in 2006. They embezzled hundreds of thousands of dollars and now they are in federal prison.

The Chicago Tribune reported that CEO Valerie Lewis stole a total of $47,238 of city, state, and federal funds in a three-year period, while executive director Patti Buffington was convicted of running a financial crime ring and stealing nearly $500,000. (2)

I donated my VCR to them, too. Now I regret that.

[Unhooked] is a voluntary program, but you get your charges expunged. So who wouldn't do it? I've talked to others who've done it and they say it wasn't too bad. They have a cop come in and do trash talk.

CCHC

I think the program has changed now, and it's a lot more negative. A friend of mine who took it said that half the class was Asian or Eastern European and didn't understand what was going on. They didn't have a translator.

[But] when people are offered a choice between having charges dropped or going through a program, in that program they're going to be put through a lot of education. In order to graduate from the program, or get to the next level, you have to admit that you were a victim.

So the question is, what is involved in this programming that gets people to start shifting their own narratives?

A new law in Illinois will create similar programming for folks facing repeat prostitution charges.

In God We Trust

End Demand
Illinois passed [a law] last year to create funding streams for "victims of sex trafficking" so to speak. They are increasing impoundment fees and fines for pimps and johns who are arrested, and creating a special license plate that you can get in Illinois. An anti-trafficking license plate.

CITY OF CHICAGO
CENTRAL
AUTO POUND
400 E. WACKER DRIVE

PA 98-1013: Funding Specialized Services for Survivors of Human Trafficking went into effect Jan. 1, 2015 with the explicit aim to support drop-in centers and emergency and long-term housing. (3)

The bill specifically instructs the Illinois Department of Human Services to consult with anti-trafficking activists, survivors, and service providers on fund expenditures, but no mention is made of speaking with sex workers' rights activists, or sex workers themselves.

Oh my god,
the day that I see one of those license plates I'm so gonna rear-end the car!

It sounds very much like Project ROSE.

A controversial collaboration between the School of Social Work at Arizona State University and the Phoenix Police Department, Project ROSE (Reaching Out to the Sexually Exploited) opened in 2011 to assist police in checking in suspects arrested in mass prostitution stings. (4)

[Sex workers] can opt to have all these services at the drop-in center, but if they don't want these services, then the police are going to press charges.

Arrestees in Project ROSE were offered a 36-week diversion program. Those ineligible or uninterested in the program faced prison time.

The problem with Project ROSE, and what it looks like would happen here, is that, if you've already done diversion, you can't do it again. Like, I've done diversion. You can only do it once.

Project ROSE was roundly criticized for violating the National Association of Social Workers' code of ethics and basic constitutional rights, prompting the ACLU to investigate. The program shut down at the end of 2014. (5)

The confusion between prostitution and trafficking doesn't just result in inconvenienced sex workers and occasional prison terms. In addition to the ethical issues it raises for social workers who may be involved, and civil rights concerns, such stings chafe against human rights regarding due legal process and free choice of employment

The Cook County Sheriff's response team performs all the arrests.

They have a team of 6 to 7 officers, and they now do all the prostitution arrests for Sheriff [Tom Dart].

There are also beat cops who, if they're driving around and see someone on the street, they can arrest them for prostitution. But the stings, where they are in a hotel and call a backpage ad—that's all done by the Human Trafficking Response Team now.

So the goal is to find people that are being trafficked, but obviously that's not always the case.

How often do you think people are referring to actual human trafficking when they say "human trafficking"?

I don't know.

The more the trafficking language is used, the more of a serious problem it sounds like, the more funding that's going to be available.

A recent study of the top 36 anti-trafficking organizations in the US indicated that they will share a budget of approximately $1.6 Billion USD this year, which is slightly higher than the GDP of Belize. (6)

A lot of [students] are working on the trafficking issue and they're very serious.

There was one girl wearing a T-shirt that said, "PIMPS: Persons Interfering with Modern Prostitution and Slavery. Change the definition." I was so excited! I said, "Oh my god, where did you get that T-shirt?" She said it was her final project for high school. They had created this campaign and made the t-shirts.

Some of them have never heard opposing viewpoints. One of them said to me [after I presented at a conference], "I used to think of this as a trafficking issue but now I think of it as a human rights issue. This is mind-fuckery!"

You're seeing younger and younger people get involved. CAASE had a bus and billboard campaign all over the city. Then you've got the celebrity angle, and these TV shows.

Prostitution. There's nothing victimless about it.

Chicago Alliance Against Sexual Exploitation (CAASE, the organization behind the End Demand Illinois campaign, launched a major ad initiative in 2013 with billboards, bus ads, and posters on garbage cans that blanketed the city with messages that erased the difference between at-will sex work and sex trafficking.

ONLY YOU CAN STOP TRAFFICKING

Grand

They are targeting young people, I think. There's the fear of someone's daughter being snatched up right out of high school and trafficked. The whole save-the-children angle, too: it's always a young girl, bound and gagged. Borderline pornographic.

It's every parent's worst nightmare. The parents get involved, and they want to educate the kids about how they can be safe, and the kids are like, "Oh my gosh! This is awful! I want to do something, I want to start my own organization!" So teenagers are starting their own anti-trafficking organizations.

But what are they *doing?* What are these organizations actually doing?

What is the biggest problem you see with the rise of anti-trafficking organizations?

Well, increased police activity. There's also the tactics of End Demand and the Swedish Model to scare away the clientele. For sex workers. that's your bread and butter.

Also there's the characterization of all people working in the sex industry as victims. It increases the negative stigma. There already is a negative stigma, but even more now.

You're a victim now.

Serpent Libertine

part II

Human trafficking legislation isn't just negatively impacting sex workers in Chicago. The same kinds of laws—End Demand laws—show up all over the country. And throughout the rest of the world.

SWOP-USA was formed in 2003.

Robyn Few was a madam in the Bay Area arrested after 9-11. A lot of madams were arrested after 9-11—the Gold Coast Madam here in Chicago, too. They were arrested under the USA PATRIOT Act. Robyn came from the medical marijuana movement and borrowed the name Sex Workers OutreachProject from an Australian organization and formed in 2003.

Stacey Swimme had formed the Desiree Alliancce, and started holding conferences. And Kitty and Betty, who formed SWOP-Chicago—I knew them. I had gone to the conference and came back to Chicago and we formed the chapter. It's very loose, grassroots stuff. It's taken awhile to build up.

The Desiree Alliance is a diverse coalition of individuals and organizations that advocate for the human and civil rights of sex workers.; SWOP-Chicago is the local affiliate of a national grassroots organization of current and former sex workers who do outreach, education, and advocacy to improve the professional and personal lives of sex workers.

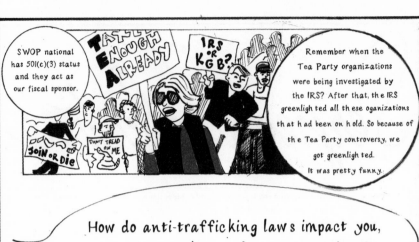

SWOP national has 501(c)(3) status and they act as our fiscal sponsor.

Remember when the Tea Party organizations were being investigated by the IRS? After that, the IRS greenlighted all these oganizations that had been on hold. So because of the Tea Party controversy, we got greenlighted. It was pretty funny.

How do anti-trafficking laws impact you, as a sex worker and as an organizer?

There have always been prostitution arrests, but we're seeing more large-scale stings. Emi Koyama has been tracking Operation Cross Country, where [the FBI is] looking to arrest pimps and johns and rescue underage sex workers, but they end up arresting a lot of consenting adult sex workers.

Emi Koyama

You see these stings used as a way to identify trafficking victims.

"While each Operation Cross Country campaign becomes bigger than the last," sex worker advocate and researcher Koyama wrote following the nationwide stings in July 2014, "the overall pattern remains the same:

"a large number of adult women in the sex trade are subject to intervention by the law enforcement (most, though not all, are arrested or cited for prostitution or other related crimes);

"young people who are trading sex in order to escape from violence at home or in the child welfare system and those who have safe homes to go back to are lumped up together and involuntarily 'rescued' back into the systems that they ran away from in the first place;

"young women and others who work with or alongside other young people are unfairly targeted as 'pimps' even when there is no sign of abuse or exploitation;

"Black and Brown men and women are profiled as 'gang members' and 'pimps' while the professionalized white rescue industry employ force, fraud, or coercion to tell young people how they should live." (2)

Also, funding. There's no funding for our organizations, unless you are going into the anti-trafficking pool of funding.

It is unclear how large that funding pool is, since government spending on anti-trafficking efforts comes from several different agencies and a full third of the largest organizations are fully funded by untrackable private money. Even the State Department's Office to Monitor and Combat Trafficking in Persons report from 2012 listed figures totaling only 1% of the government funding available to support anti-trafficking work than when compared to individual organizations's 990s. (3)

For our organization, it is a little scary because if you're aware of somebody under the age of 18 performing any form of sexual services, whether they're consenting to it or not, and you don't report it to authorities, you can be charged with trafficking.

I don't know the likelihood of that actually happening, but that is a concern with a lot of the organizations that work with youth.

Publicly citing funding difficulties, the Young Women's Empowerment Project (YWEP) in Chicago—an organization that worked with young people of color in the sex trade and street economies—shut down in 2013. Rumors abound, however, that the organization simply feared legal prosecution, and a vital resource for street workers was lost.

Do you have difficulty finding members?

I think a lot of sex worker's rights organizations do. Usually people who work in the industry are not activists. When they get arrested, it can be a catalyst.

There's such a wide variety of issues [in the sex trade]. With the lack of funding, it's hard to determine the issues that are most important to sex workers.

We try to do workshops and outreach, but the industry is so large and so broad that it's hard to really focus on one particular area or population.

Sex work can include jobs in porn, strip clubs, or direct sexual services, so the range of protections workers require is vast.

It's hard to work on policy because, when you're dealing with people who are still in the industry, making friends with legislators and policy makers is tough. They don't want to associate with a criminalized part of the population. We've seen a lot of progress in the war on drugs, but it's still hard with prostitution and sex work. Especially with the trafficking thing. You can't compete with the down-and-out stories.

That's one thing I realized: they're appealing to people's greatest fears. That their brother / sister / daughter / son is going to be snatched up. Trafficked. Everyone loves a sob story.

I've seen a couple of these presentations where a couple of women get up and tell their story, and the story sounds very coached.

International Justice Mission (IJM) had a symposium at this megachurch near Old Town, and this woman gets up and says,

"I RAN AWAY FROM HOME AND WITHIN AN HOUR I WAS SNATCHED UP OFF THE STREET BY A TRAFFICKER AND I WAS FORCED TO HAVE SEX WITH HUNDREDS OF MEN... AND THEN I ESCAPED..."

All the elements of a perfect story.

I just don't think it's always like that.

The *Taken* movie is a perfect example, with Liam Neeson. The guy said it was a true story: He was on vacation with his daughter and she was taken by a trafficking ring and it turns out it was all a lie. And they made this major motion picture! Three of them!

In 2011, the Attorney's Office issued a press release regarding the author of the story: "[William] Hillar fabricated a gruesome tale that his own daughter had been kidnapped, forced into sex slavery, sodomized, and tortured before being hacked to death with machetes and thrown into the sea...Hillard admits that he fabricated the story about his daughter, who was alive and well.' (4)

The IJM thing was a couple years ago. Someone else had seen the same survivor speak a couple years later and said she had gotten emotional at all the same moments, and told the story in the same way. I don't want to disrespect someone's story, but everything about it is what we've heard before.

All the elements of the perfect sex-trafficking horror story, and then she escaped, and then here she is, telling her story. I've just seen that several times, the story that seems like it's been written. I don't want to say, "I don't believe your story."

We just don't know.

A really good example of this was at a harm-reduction conference [where SWOP presented.] There was a woman there who had attended all the sex-work related presentations. Every time she raised her hand to ask a question, she would immediately start off with,

She would always preface her question with that.

"MY NAME IS SUCH AND SUCH. I WAS A TRAFFICKING VICTIM FROM 2004-2011, AND..."

I wonder if a true victim of trafficking would want to announce that to the world, over and over again? But there is this weird sense of pride in being able to say, "I overcame this. This is the hot-button issue and, look at me, now I'm doing this work."

When you attend a conference it's very strange to do that. Every time she spoke, everyone would be dangling on her words, because she'd set herself up that way.

It's just like Somaly Mam.

Now disgraced Cambodian sex-trafficking victim advocate, Somaly Mam has been accused of deflecting criticism by claiming victimhood. In many instances, she does exactly that, responding to proof of her own falsehoods by stating that, for example, "most" of the girls in her AFESIP shelters were trafficked, when according to their own reports, the majority of them were at-will sex workers. (5)

What happens when you talk directly to folks who identify as victims?

Well, I'll tell you a very awkward thing. Amnesty International had their national conference here in April, a meeting that included looking at a policy proposal—*only a proposal*—to support the decriminilization of prostitution as a human rights issue. It has not been voted on yet, and god only knows if it will ever be voted on.

CAASE and the End Demand people came out and protested the hotel. SWOP was always planning to go and show support. It was just an hour-long session where they talked about the proposal, but CAASE was protesting. They brought all these signs, and they brought Lisa Madigan. She was speaking in front of the hotel, and we were there. So we had a protest in front of the hotel. Which we weren't really intending to do; but they had all these people with signs, saying, "Don't decriminalize pimps and johns." They got all this press.

J.W. MARRIOTT

PROSTITUTION IS VIOLENCE

NO

END NOW

DO NOT DECRIMINALIZE PIMPS & JOHNS

STOP IT

REAL MEN DON'T BUY SEX

END DEMAND

"Amnesty says its organization's internal debate over decriminalization centers on sex workers involved in consensual sex, not sex trafficking and child sex abuse," a *Sun Times* reporter noted. (6)

(Amnesty International later announced they would like to vote on the proposal in August 2015, which prompted more protest and outrage: this time from Hollywood stars like Meryl Streep and Emma Thompson, whose self-proclaimed expertise came from acting as sex workers in blockbuster films. The proposal to support decriminalization, however, relied on years of study about the ineffectiveness of the so-called Swedish Model/End Demand policy and the human rights abuses it consistently seems to allow for.)

At one point [at the protest], one of the board members from Amnesty brought over a couple of the survivors that were there with CAASE and introduced us, right on the sidewalk. It was very bizarre.

One of them asked me, straight to my face, "Are you a sex worker?"—well, she wouldn't have used the term sex worker, since they're very opposed to that terminology. She asked if I worked in the sex trade.

"YES, I AM. I HAVE BEEN FOR YEARS."

"I UNDERSTAND. I USED TO BE LIKE YOU."

"WELL, I'M NOT GONNA CHANGE"

It was not the time or place to have that discussion, and one of the other SWOP members said, "This is getting kind of awkward."

Anti-trafficking organizations train folks to approach women in the sex industry as if women engaged in commercial sex are fundamentally incapable of understanding their own situations, as if they all have Stockholm Syndrome. It seems almost infantilizing.

Exactly.

That's how I felt when I was approached by this woman.

And that language- "prostituted person" —that's not person-first language. Why aren't they using person-first language?

What ended up happening was, CAASE met with the board of Amnesty. Then someone from Amnesty said, well, if we're going to meet with the anti-trafficking folks, then we need to meet with the sex workers' rights people, so several of us had a meeting with the members of the board. We actually got the last word.

So Amnesty International even noted how important the stories are. Have you ever felt pressured to reframe your own narrative?

Oh absolutely. [When I went through the Unhooked program] I was an undergrad and I said something like, "Well I'm in college and I have rent and bills to pay..." whatever I was explaining.

The woman running the group said, "Well if you didn't have to pay tuition would you be doing this?" She was challenging the need for money, basically.

In the group I said, "I don't have any issues with it." At the time, I hadn't had any bad experiences. Getting arrested was the worst experience I'd ever had.

Sounds like she wanted you to admit that if money weren't an issue, you'd do something else. The only problem is that money is an issue. Seems like a common thread that runs through a lot of arguments for End Demand legislation: no little girl wants to grow up to be a prostitute.

The one thing these bills did do is eliminate felony prostitution. It's hard to say that's not an advancement. But what you're trying to do, the ultimate goal.... you may win a few battles but you're going to lose the war.

You're not going to be able to end demand for sexual services. No matter how hard you try.

The first bill CAASE passed was called the Illinois Safe Children Act. Nobody's gonna argue against that. I mean, all this stuff on paper— what policy maker would argue with any of it?

We went and lobbied against the bill and we were laughed at. A woman let us into her office but only becasue there's an organization called the South West Organizing Project, also called SWOP, and she thought that's where we were from. But she said,

"ITS GOOD WE HAVE PEOPLE LIKE YOU TO TELL US ABOUT THIS LEGISLATION. WE DON'T KNOW ANYTHING ABOUT IT UNTIL WE HAVE SOMEONE IN OUR OFFICE.

Part of the problem, too, is what they're spending money on. The "Ugly Truth" campaign was a really good example. Why are you spending all this money on this campaign when that could be going toward services, housing?

Every single conference I go to, the Cook County folks are always talking about the lack of beds for juvenile trafficking victims. There's no housing.

143

Then there are real questions about the economics behind End Demand policies.

It's super complicated, but how I have explained it is, if there are five johns and five sex workers, then... whatever. But then End Demand comes along, so there are two johns and five sex workers, but those five sex workers still need to make the same amount of money, whether they are a trafficking victim or not.

In targeting johns, End Demand may keep some men away from sex workers, but it doesn't change the needs of the workers.

So all these five people are competing for these two johns, and the johns are saying,

WELL, THIS GIRL WILL DO ME FOR A HUNDRED DOLLARS AND YOU'RE TRYING TO CHARGE ME TWO HUNDRED DOLLARS, SO WHAT WILL YOU DO FOR ME FOR THAT MUCH?

That's what I try to explain to anti-trafficking students: regardless of whether or not you think sex work should go on, we're talking about individuals who have to make this money, whether they're consenting or being forced.

Basically what it would do is, everybody would lower their price, and the demand will actually increase because everybody lowers their price.

Didn't Emi Koyama also suggest that the two johns left over after End Demand/Swedish Model laws pass are going to be higher risk takers and potentially more violent clients?

Pye Jakobsson, the president of the Network of Sex Work Projects, has a video where she explains what happened in Sweden when they first enacted the Swedish Model.

Actually demand didn't go away, but the workers in the street economy—all their screening techniques were taken away because the clients were like, "Hey, you have nothing to lose, I do: either do what I ask and I'll give you this amount of money or I'm going to go down the street and I'll get the next girl to do whatever."

They knew that the demand had decreased, so they had the upper hand in the transaction. That's how she explained it.

Yet End Demand supporters seem to think similar legislation will resolve human trafficking in the US.

The IJM event was at this megachurch. It was huge! It had its own coffeeshop and everything. This politician, Peter Roskam from the suburbs, the sixth congressional district, got up and said,

WHAT IS THE SOLUTION FOR TRAFFICKING?

WELL THE SOLUTION FOR TRAFFICKING IS FOR THE TRAFFICKERS TO FIND THE LORD JESUS CHRIST.

It's so simple.

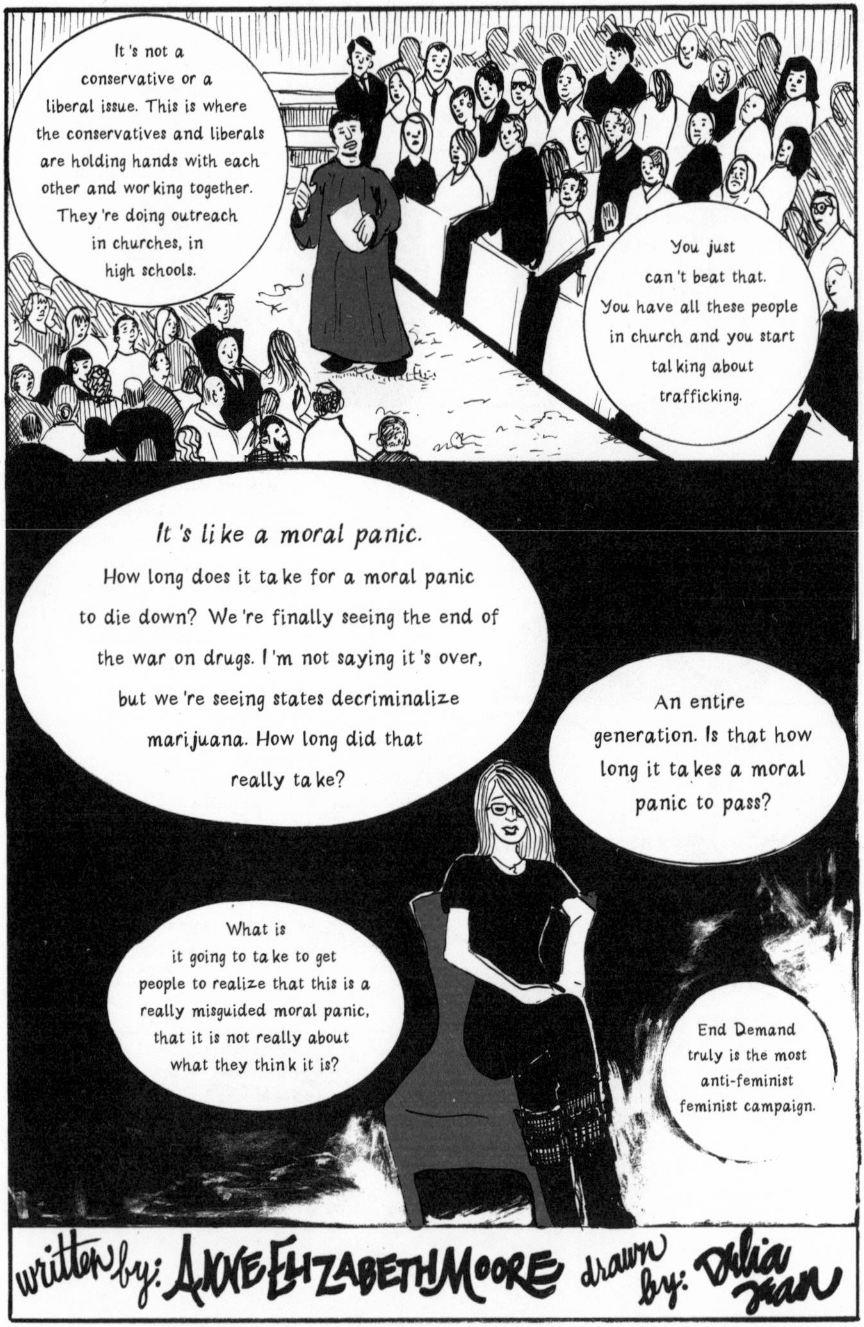
It's not a conservative or a liberal issue. This is where the conservatives and liberals are holding hands with each other and working together. They're doing outreach in churches, in high schools.
You just can't beat that. You have all these people in church and you start talking about trafficking.
It's like a moral panic. How long does it take for a moral panic to die down? We're finally seeing the end of the war on drugs. I'm not saying it's over, but we're seeing states decriminalize marijuana. How long did that really take?
An entire generation. Is that how long it takes a moral panic to pass?
What is it going to take to get people to realize that this is a really misguided moral panic, that it is not really about what they think it is?
End Demand truly is the most anti-feminist feminist campaign.
written by: ANNE ELIZABETH MOORE drawn by: Dalia Jean

As we've seen, estimated numbers of human trafficking victims are regularly 60 to 100 times the documented figures.

NGO funding, intended to "free" victims of human trafficking, can go toward religious instruction and limited work opportunities that challenge the notion of freedom.

The Connecting Threads

WRITTEN BY ANNE ELIZABETH MOORE
DRAWN BY LEELA CORMAN

At-will sex-workers are locked up in brothel raids abroad, and here in the US, under new, not dissimilar, legislation.

Workers at every stage of apparel production and distribution, from modeling to offshore product manufacturing, suffer low wages, sexual harassment, and hostile work environments ranging from insufficient health care to worker shootings...

... all made possible by US and EU policy agreements that range in application from trafficking-in-persons legislation to IP mandates,

And the companies that fund organizations to put women back on the factory line often profit directly from their labor.

... It may start to feel like the global economic condition of women is both permanent and natural, and nothing you can do will make any difference.

Apparently it's about more than just ending sex trafficking and buying sweat-free?

Remember, the fashion industry employs one in seven women worldwide, and there are no reliable estimates of how many women in the world—cis or trans—work in the sex industry.

$10, please.

We do know that policing of and conditions within the sex and garment industries severely limit women's potential for economic justice.

APECRUMMY & FILCH Clothing

CHEAP

So if you want to support job opportunities for women in developing nations, don't shop at the mall.

If you're concerned about human trafficking, don't go on an NGO brothel tour. Advocate for a living wage in the garment industry.

Support local sex workers' rights organizations, hold retailers responsible for warehouse labor conditions, and demand trade policies that include strong, incentivized health and safety provisions.

Warmart

R WAGES R WAG

And run for office.

The global economic condition of women isn't a "consumer awareness" problem, nor was it created—or is it solveable—by any one person. The global economic condition of women is caused by bad policy.

And policy can, and must, change.

Endnotes for Chapter Four

The Somaly Problem

1. The Somaly Mam Foundation shut down at the end of 2014, after the *Newsweek* article appeared. When Mam revived the foundation a year later, she changed its name to the New Somaly Mam Foundation, although little else had changed: the website even featured pictures of former AFESIP residents, at least one of whose stories has also been challenged as untruthful. (Although it was widely claimed that this article was the first appearance of such allegations against Mam, they had been included in Moore's 2012 *Baffler* article on Nicholas Kristof's *Half the Sky*, "Marketpiece Theater," available online at http://thebaffler.com/salvos/marketpiece-theater.)

2. Irin Carmon. "Nick Kristof to the Rescue!," *Salon.com* (November 8, 2011). http://salon.com/2011/11/08/nick_kristof_to_the_rescue/ (accessed June 2, 2014). Also pointed out in the *Baffler* piece noted above, posting pictures of young women online without their permission may be tasteless and unethical, but Kristof's previous purchase of two supposed sex slaves was a violation of local and international laws, crimes for which he has never been held accountable.

3. "FAQ," Love 146 website. http://love146.org/faqs/ (accessed April 22, 2014).

4. "20 People say 'yes' to Jesus at AEC," AIM Quarterly Update, Agape International Mission website. http://agapewebsite.org/updatesummer2014/#2 (accessed October 14, 2015).

5. Eric Campano. "Are Evangelicals Monopolizing, Misleading U.S. Anti-Trafficking Efforts?," *Patheos.com* (January 17, 2013). Http://www.patheos.com/blogs/religionnow/2013/01/are-evangelicals-monopolizing-misleading-us-anti-trafficking-efforts/ (accessed June 20, 2014).

6. Cambodia figures from 2011 and 2014. Julia Wallace and Kuch Naren, "How bad is sex trafficking in Cambodia?" *Al Jazeera* (June 9, 2014).

http://www.aljazeera.com/indepth/features/2014/06/how-bad-sex-trafficking-cambodia-201468124236117557.html (accessed October 14, 2015). U.S. numbers are from State Department estimates 2002-2010, as cited in Willoughby Mariano, "Despite millions spent, human trafficking's scope is unknown." *Atlanta Journal-Constitution* (December 31, 2012). http://www. ajc.com/news/news/despite-millions-spent-human-traffickings-scope-is/ nTjRn/ (accessed October 14, 2015). Global figure from the ILO's report, *Global Alliance Against Forced Labor*, from 2005, online at Http://www.ilo. org/global/publications/magazines-and-journals/world-of-work-magazine/ articles/WCMS_081360/lang--en/index.htm (accessed October 14, 2015).

7. That's 3397 global and 2645 domestic clients served, to be exact, which you'll want to weigh against the above numbers of documented trafficking victims. From the Love 146 *Total Child Impact Report* 2012–2013. http:// love146.org/wp-content/uploads/2013/06/Love146_Impact-Report-2012-13. pdf (accessed October 14, 2015).

8. Melissa Gira Grant. "Fighting sex trafficking with Jesus." *Salon.com* (April 27, 2014). Http://www.salon.com/2014/04/27/fighting_sex_trafficking_ with_jesus_how_the_religious_rights_healing_hurts/ (accessed October 14, 2015).

Unraveling

1. As told to Vivian Ho in "Closure of prostitution website costly for sex workers," *SFGate*, 15 July, 2014. http://www.sfgate.com/crime/article/ Closure-of-prostitution-website-costly-for-sex-5619118.php (accessed July 15, 2015).

2. Ibid.

3. "Internet Based," The Polaris Project website. http://www.polarisproject. org/human-trafficking/sex-trafficking-in-the-us/internet-based (accessed July 15, 2015).

4. "Projects," CATW website. http://catwinternational.org/ ProjectsCampaigns/Projects (accessed July 15).

5. "AFESIP Cambodia Annual Report 2012" AFESIP Cambodia, Phnom Penh (2013). http://www.afesip.org/about-us/annual-report (accessed October 14, 2015).

6. "Combined financial statements year ended December 31, 2012," Somaly Mam Foundation, Phnom Penh, Cambodia (2013). This form is not currently available on the New Somaly Mam Foundation's website.

7. "Annual Report 2013," International Justice Mission, Washington DC (2014). https://www.ijm.org/content/2013-annual-report (accessed October 14, 2015).

8. "Annual Report 2013," Shared Hope International, Arlington, VA (2014). http://sharedhope.org/wp-content/uploads/2014/04/Shared-Hope-Annual-Report-2013.pdf (accessed October 14, 2015).

9. From the Shared Hope International mission statement. http://sharedhope.org/about-us/our-mission-and-values/ (accessed October 14, 2015).

Serpent Libertine, Part I

1. Unless otherwise attributed, all Libertine's quotes come from an in-person interview with Anne Elizabeth Moore and Delia Jean recorded on January 2, 2015.

2. Carlos Sadovi. "2 officials of home to help prostitutes charged in scam," *Chicago Tribune*, October 4, 2006. http://articles.chicagotribune.com/2006-10-04/news/0610040049_1_lavish-prosecutors-richard-devine (accessed Mar. 2, 2015).

3. "PA 98-1013: Funding Specialized Services for Survivors of Human Trafficking– Summary," End Demand Illinois, August 21, 2014. http://media.virbcdn.com/files/f7/6ea26df7378b1945-ILSB3558BillSummaryFINAL.pdf (accessed Mar. 2, 2015).

4. Leandra Huffner. "ASU collaboration provides alternatives for prostitutes," *The State Press*, October 10, 2011. Http://www.statepress.com/2011/10/10/asu-collaboration-provides-alternatives-for-prostitutes/ (accessed March 12, 2015).

5. "Project ROSE stings end in Phoenix, AZ, Monica Jones responds," *Best Practices Policy*, November 27, 2014. http://www.bestpracticespolicy.org/2014/11/27/breaking-news-from-arizona/ (Accessed March 12, 2015).

6. Anne Elizabeth Moore. "The American Rescue Industry," *Truthout* (April 8, 2015). http://www.truth-out.org/news/item/30060-the-american-rescue-industry-toward-an-anti-trafficking-paramilitary (accessed October 14, 2015). "A programmatic overview of self-reported documents from the 36 biggest anti-trafficking organizations in the United States makes clear that the American rescue industry is white male-led," that report notes, "and focused on intervening in a predominantly female population (many of whom are women of color) without regard to this population's post-rescue needs, the effectiveness of the organization's efforts or the framing of human trafficking in general. ... Unfortunately, this is not some speculative, crackpot conspiracy theory: White men in the United States really are receiving government and private funds that they're failing to fully account for to arrest or detain women with little regard to their needs or interests; some are even doing so as extremely well-funded and popularly supported guerilla groups. Indeed, the quasi-governmental tendencies of anti-trafficking organizations lend the American rescue industry in sum the sheen of a paramilitary force, operating under a handshake agreement with elected officials to push through unpalatable legislation."

Serpent Libertine, Part II

1. Unless otherwise attributed, all Libertine's quotes come from an in-person interview with Anne Elizabeth Moore and Delia Jean recorded on January 2, 2015.

2. Emi Koyama. "Operation Cross Country VII: Roundup and Comments," *Eminism*, July 3, 2014. http://eminism.org/blog/entry/429 (accessed March 12, 2015).

3. Anne Elizabeth Moore. "The American Rescue Industry," *Truthout* (April 8, 2015). http://www.truth-out.org/news/item/30060-the-american-rescue-industry-toward-an-anti-trafficking-paramilitary (accessed October 14, 2015).

4. "Millersville man sentenced for posing as a retired Army Special Forces colonel," U.S. Attorney's Office, Baltimore, Maryland, August 30, 2011. http://www.fbi.gov/baltimore/press-releases/2011/millersville-man-sentenced-for-posing-as-a-retired-army-special-forces-colonel (accessed March 12, 2015).

5. Maudlyn Ihejirika. "Protesters rally against sex-work discussion," April 5, 2014, *Chicago Sun-Times*. http://chicago.suntimes.com/uncategorized/7/71/194836/protesters-rally-against-sex-work-discussion/ (accessed March 12, 2015). On August 11, 2015, Amnesty International met in Dublin and voted to push for the decriminalization of sex work as a human rights issue. While the move sparked outcry—notably from a contingent of Hollywood actresses—and more thoughtful debate, it furthered an ongoing global discussion about women's human rights in all fields of labor.

About the Ladydrawers

The Ladydrawers Comics Collective (AKA "the Ladydrawers") is an unofficially affiliated group of female-, male- and non-binary gender identified folk who research, perform, create and publish accessible comics, texts, and films about how economics, race, sexuality, and gender impact the comics industry, other media, and our culture at large. Our data comes from original research conducted in the public realm by students, interns, volunteers, supporters, and professionals around the globe. Our content—including comic books, strips, posters, postcards, games, videos, films, performances, and apparel—is created by a range of folks interested in, and with a range of experiences in, the comics industry, including long-time, established professionals as well as recent enthusiasts. Together we are a curiosity-driven, open-ended, exploratory body of friendly and talented researchers, concerned with who gets to say what in our culture and how they may or may not be supported in or compensated for saying it. Our monthly comic strips at *Bitch* and *Truthout*, which draw between several thousand to nearly a hundred thousand readers, both document and illustrate our findings for the public at large; our projects also pay underrepresented artists to make comics in a field in which it can be difficult to make money as a woman, nonbinary person, or person of color.

In April of 2010, we published our first data set on women's comics anthologies in a pamphlet called *Women's Comics Anthology*; we conducted an internationally debated postcard campaign in May of 2011; released a limited-edition print anthology now available online in July of 2011 called *Unladylike*; and put out a book in conjunction with the Adventure School in June of 2012 called *Hand Job: A Labor of Love*. Our projects have been commissioned by *Tin House* and *Annalemma*, and appear in monthly columns on *Truthout* and *Bitch*. Using a strategy combining friendliness, charm, jokes, data, and cats, we have conducted projects in conjunction with Our Bodies Ourselves and other social-justice minded, information-disseminating organizations, and at the Museum of Contemporary Art in Chicago. We have held educational programs at School of the Art Institute of Chicago and the Ox-Bow School of Art, and given presentations at Northwestern University's Sex Week, the Chicago Alternative Comics Expo (CAKE), the Chicago Cultural Center (for the Chicago Department of Cultural Affairs and Chicago Artists' Resource), at the Cambodian Association of Illinois, and at the Pop Culture and World Politics Conference at Hobart and William Smith Colleges in Geneva, New York. We've been honored to show this work at Pilsen's Uri-Eichen gallery in Chicago, and to take it on a genuine world tour, delivering talks on it in art spaces and at universities in Newcastle and London, England; Helsinki, Finland; Vienna, Austria; Phnom Penh, Cambodia; and Chicago, New York City, and Los Angeles in the U.S. In 2012, we implemented a two-week experimental graduate program with the Adventure School for Ladies called the Comics Intensive, and conducted a three-day seminar based on the same principles at the Comics Center in Helsinki, Finland in 2014. In the summer of 2013, under a residency at the A+D Gallery at Columbia College, we led a summer-long series including an art exhibition and free workshops called SEX. MONEY. RACE. GENDER.: The Ladydrawers (of Chicago, Ill.) that explored how identity politics operate under capitalism. In the coming year, we will release our successfully Kickstarter-funded documentary *Comics Undressed*, on gender, racial, and sexual diversity in the comics industry.

Creator Biographies

Leela Corman's illustrations have appeared in the New York *Times*, *Boston Phoenix*, *Lilith*, *Bust*, and *Tikkun*. Her comics have appeared in *Heeb Magazine*, *Quadrado*, *Scheherazade*, and *PULSE! Magazine*, and have been translated into French and Portuguese. Her award-winning graphic novels include the self-published *Queen's Day*, the teen-angst tale *Subway Series* (Alternative Comics), and the critically lauded *Unterzakhn* (Schocken). She studied painting, printmaking, and illustration at Massachusetts College of Art. She is also a professional bellydancer. She lives in Gainesville, Florida with her husband and daughter.

Julia Gfrörer was born in 1982 in Concord, New Hampshire. Her work has appeared in *Thickness*, *Arthur Magazine*, *Study Group Magazine*, *Black Eye*, and *Best American Comics*. Her graphic novel, *Black is the Color* (Fantagraphics) has been widely acclaimed.

Simon Häussle is a Vienna-based artist and comics creator. He is part of Tonto Comics as well as the Kabinett Passage exhibition space at MQ in Vienna. See work in process at: www.simonshaus.wordpress.com

Delia Jean began her highly lauded, self-published comics series *Station in Life*, about women's labor in the service sector, when she was working in the food-service industry in downtown Chicago. After a brief respite on the East Coast, she has returned to the city and the comics lifestyle.

Born on Long Island, illustrator and writer Ellen Lindner is the author of *Undertow* (Soaring Penguin Press), a graphic novel about Coney Island in the early 1960s, and the editor of *The Strumpet*, a transatlantic comics magazine showcasing art by upcoming women cartoonists.

Melissa Mendes is a cartoonist and illustrator. She lives and works in Hancock, MA. She is the creator of *Freddy Stories*, *Joey*, and *Lou*, from Oily Comics. She is self-publishing *The Weight*, an epic family saga inspired by her grandfather's life set in rural New York state, spanning from the 1930s onward. You can find out more about her at www. Mmmendes.com

Award-winning journalist and bestselling comics anthologist Anne Elizabeth Moore was born in Winner, SD and grew up in St. Paul, MN. Currently in Chicago, she is the author of *Unmarketable* from the New Press (Best Book, *Mother Jones*) and a series of memoirs from Cantankerous Titles including *New Girl Law* and *Cambodian Grrrl* (Best Book, Lowell Thomas Travel Journalism Award). She is the former editor of *Punk Planet*, *The Comics Journal*, and the *Best American Comics* series from Houghton Mifflin. Her cultural criticism has appeared in *The Baffler*, *The New Inquiry*, *Jacobin*, *Tin House*, *Salon*, *TPM*, *Truthout*, and *Al Jazeera*. Her work has been featured in *The Guardian*, *The New York Times*, *The Village Voice*, *Entertainment Weekly*, *The Chicago Reader*, and many others, and she has appeared on *CNN*, *WTTW*, *WBEZ*, *WNUR*, *Radio Australia*, and *Voice of America*. She is a Fulbright scholar and the recipient of a USC Annenberg Getty Arts Journalism Fellowship and an Arthur and Lila Weinberg Fellowship at the Newberry Library. She has two cats and teaches at the School of the Art Institute of Chicago.

SUBSCRIBE TO EVERYTHING WE PUBLISH!

Do you love what Microcosm publishes?

Do you want us to publish more great stuff?

Would you like to receive each new title as it's published?

Subscribe as a BFF to our new titles and we'll mail them all to you as they are released!

$10-30/mo, pay what you can afford. Include your t-shirt size and month/date of birthday for a possible surprise! Subscription begins the month after it is purchased.

microcosmpublishing.com/bff

...AND HELP US GROW YOUR SMALL WORLD!

...and check out our other fine works of comics journalism: